NO TIME
LIKE THE FUTURE

Also by Michael J. Fox

Lucky Man: A Memoir

Always Looking Up: The Adventures of an Incurable Optimist

A Funny Thing Happened on the Way to the Future

NO TIME
LIKE THE FUTURE

AN OPTIMIST
CONSIDERS MORTALITY

———

MICHAEL J. FOX

HEADLINE

The right of Michael J Fox to be identified as the Author of
the Work has been asserted by him in accordance with the
Copyright, Designs and Patents Act 1988.

First published in Great Britain in 2020 by
HEADLINE PUBLISHING GROUP

First published in the US in 2020 by
FLATIRON BOOKS

1

Book design by Michelle McMillian
Chapter opener illustrations by Rhys Davies

Every effort has been made to fulfil requirements with regard to reproducing copyright material.
The author and publisher will be glad to rectify any omissions at the earliest opportunity.

Cataloguing in Publication Data is available from the British Library

Hardback ISBN 978 1 4722 7846 3
Trade paperback ISBN 978 1 4722 7847 0

Offset in 11.5/17pt Fournier MT Std by Jouve (UK), Milton Keynes

Printed and bound in Great Britain by Clays Ltd, Elcograf S.p.A.

Headline's policy is to use papers that are natural, renewable and recyclable
products and made from wood grown in well-managed forests and other
controlled sources. The logging and manufacturing processes are expected
to conform to the environmental regulations of the country of origin.

HEADLINE PUBLISHING GROUP
An Hachette UK Company
Carmelite House
50 Victoria Embankment
London EC4Y 0DZ

www.headline.co.uk
www.hachette.co.uk

For
Stephen, Gary,
Nanci, and Bob.
Gratitude.

Contents

"Ever since Michael J. Fox went public with his diagnosis in 1998, his life has looked, from afar anyway, almost charmed. The foundation he started has raised a staggering $800 million to combat Parkinson's disease. He's written three best-selling memoirs and even continued to act, in substantive roles. His family life, with his wife of three decades, Tracy Pollan, is by all accounts a dream. His was a remarkably positive second act."

—David Marchese, *The New York Times Magazine*, March 1, 2019

"The world eventually sends out a mean-ass Patrol Boy to slow your progress and show you who's boss."

—Stephen King, *The Dark Tower: The Gunslinger*

NO TIME
LIKE THE FUTURE

Introduction

FALL GUY

August 13, 2018, 6:30 a.m.

I'm going down. It's a flash fall. Vertical to horizontal in a blink. I twist my head to save my face from collision with the kitchen tile. What the hell just happened? I rise up on my right elbow, expecting to shift my weight to the left and push up onto my feet. Surprise: I can't feel my left arm. As my shock subsides, it's clear that I need help. Slithering forward on my belly toward the wall-mounted phone, I am a one-armed commando crawling under the table, across the floor, and through a thicket of chair legs, dragging a sandbag of a left arm that remains unresponsive and unavailable.

───

After thirty years of Parkinson's, I have established a sort of détente with the disease. We've had a history together. I've long realized that control is out of the question; instead, I've settled for an understanding that requires adaptability and resilience. PD is like the persistent and cutting jab of a boxer, manageable if I'm willing to do a little feinting and weaving. But then came the check hook; the blow that put me on my knees for a while. Unrelated to PD, a tumor had been found high on my spinal cord. The mass was benign, but constricting, and well on its way to leaving me paralyzed. Menacing all on its own, the defect necessitated high-risk surgery, which was completed just four months prior to this moment on the kitchen floor. Through the crucible of recovery and rehabilitation, I have gone from wheelchair to walker to cane to, at last, walking. And then this happened.

The day before the accident, I flew back to Manhattan from Martha's Vineyard, in the middle of our summer vacation. Tracy was concerned about me staying in New York by myself. I was still what we would both describe as "a little wobbly on my feet." But I'd been asked to do a one-day cameo on a Spike Lee–produced movie, up in the Bronx, and it offered a brief window of independence. "I'll be back in two days," I promised. "Save me a lobster."

Schuyler, one of our twenty-five-year-old twin daughters, also needed to head back to the city for work, so we traveled home together. She lingered with me for dinner, take-out pasta at the kitchen table. Polishing off the last forkful, she had a question.

"How do you feel about going back to work?"

"I don't know, I guess I feel normal again."

"But are you *nervous*, Dood?" All of my kids call me that. Not Dude, *Dood*.

I flashed a confident smile. "Hey, it's my job. It's what I do."

Sky offered to stay over in her old room, in case I needed her to fix breakfast in the morning or to help me get organized before leaving for the set. "Skeeter, I love you. I've done this a million times. You go back to your apartment, get some rest. I'll be fine."

"Okay," she said, "but promise me you won't . . ."

I finished her sentence ". . . walk with my cell phone."

She smiled. It was a gentle reprimand, and deserved. I am an expert at walking and chewing gum at the same time, but the consensus is that I'm incapable of doing it safely with a phone in my hand. It wreaks havoc with my coordination.

"You got it."

I hugged her good night and watched the elevator doors close. For the first time in months, I was alone.

Whatever it was that brought me down, it brought me down hard and in a hurry. *I have fallen and*—like that pitiable older woman splayed at the foot of the staircase, next to an upended laundry basket—*I can't get up*. I have a theory about pain: If an injury hurts immediately, I know for sure it's benign; but pain that intensifies after a few minutes is reporting real damage.

And now, here comes the pain.

A tiny transfer of weight to my left summons two revelations. One, a sleeve of hurt rockets down my useless arm; and two, I realize that my cell phone is in my pocket. I slipped it into the back of my sweatpants before I came into the kitchen. (*Note to Schuyler: It wasn't in my hand*). My first instinct is to call Tracy, but she is five hours away on Martha's Vineyard, and I don't want to freak her out. Instead, I call my assistant, Nina, who jumps in a taxi and is on her way within minutes.

Oddly, I think of Jimmy Cagney, of all people. He once sent me a note on the first day of a new movie. *Be on time, know your lines, and don't bump into the furniture*. This morning, I was on schedule and I knew my two pages of dialogue, but the third point was a colossal fail.

While I wait for Nina, I slump on the kitchen floor, pissed off, my misery multiplying exponentially. I try to make sense out of this shit-show, but none of my all-purpose bromides and affirmations serve the moment. There is no spinning this. It's just pain and regret. There is no finding the positive and moving on to the next circumstance life has to offer. I feel something beyond frustration and anger, something akin to shame: embarrassment. Every day since the spinal cord surgery in April, everyone—doctors, family members, and friends—have repeated this message to me over and over. *You have one job: Don't fall.* Yet here I am.

This incident on the kitchen floor brings me down in more ways than one. It isn't that I am hurt; I've been hurt many times. I've been through a lot, suffered the slings and arrows. But for some reason, this just feels personal.

Make lemons into lemonade? Screw it—I'm out of the lemonade business.

FAMILY MAN

Sam is the only one of our children born before my Parkinson's diagnosis. I'm sure he has no memories in that context; he probably wasn't even aware. I did the basic dad stuff: caught frogs at the pond; tagged along to the Mommy & Me music classes, with the Orff instruments and the super-serious nannies; and tried to interest him in team sports, which was a no-go (too much arguing). I showed Sam how to tie his shoes, using the rabbit method: one ear goes up, the other lace lassoes that ear, slips under the loop, and becomes the second ear. I taught him how to ride a bike, gently pushing from behind as he found the confidence to press the pedals and gather speed. Now, on occasion, Sam pushes me—in a wheelchair. On my end, no pedaling is required. When I rise carefully from the chair, my son often checks my laces before I take a step, and he's quick to tie them for me, if needed.

The only problem for my firstborn was a matter of timing. More consequential to his life than my still-developing Parkinson's disease was another timeline—Sam was born three years before I gave up drinking, a sobriety that I still maintain. Too much of our father/child pre-K quality time was "Miller Time." He tells me that his earliest memories include going to the fridge to get me beers. I can't recall my drinking ever putting Sam or Tracy in jeopardy, but alcohol was an evolving problem.

I had been adamant that we have a child early in our marriage, very much fixated on the archetypal husband/father. Any space put between these two was too big of a space; to be a husband and not a father didn't make sense to me. I'm sure Tracy conveyed reluctance or hesitation, but I failed to read her true feelings and to understand how severely maternity would disrupt her ascending career.

There were repercussions to these first few faulty steps; we found ourselves on infirm ground. I was engaged as a dad and I loved my son, but in some ways, I was only going through the motions of being a dad. For as sanguine an adult as Sam is now, his early childhood was fraught with challenges. He was colicky and unusually glum for a child that young. I was of little help. Plus, I was drinking, and with news of my Parkinson's diagnosis, inner turmoil met outer tremulousness. Something had to give.

So logically, my suggestion to Tracy was that we have another child. She shook her head, incredulous. "Are you joking?" Her resistance had little to do with any theretofore-unproven concerns about hereditary Parkinson's disease, or my ability to function as a potentially disabled parent. Instead, it had everything to do with my drinking and my state of mind, which at that point was in survival mode. I was often traveling for work, but my isolation on the road was no more profound than my growing sense of isolation at home. I felt marginalized in a way, not understanding that I was the instrument of that detachment. I was moody, confused about the status of our marriage, the direction of my career, and—given my recent diagnosis—the future existence of a career at all.

Finally, after one particularly nasty night of drinking, I awoke to find Tracy standing over me as I slept on the couch, a spilled beer on the carpet next to my draping arm. She took in the scene and simply asked me, "Is this what you want?" It wasn't anger in her voice that caused me right then and there to change my life forever. It was boredom. She scared the hell out of me. Tracy was so over this whole floor show.

I committed to regularly attending a 12-step program, and I enlisted Joyce, a gifted Jungian analyst, who helped me put out the fires, as she would do many more times throughout the years. Gradually, I learned to accept and understand my new illness. I could put down a drink, but Parkinson's would be with me for the rest of my life. The knowledge, tools, and counseling that the program provided also served to illuminate a path forward with my disease. I worked hard on not just becoming my old self again, but a newer, better version.

Six years after our wedding, four years after I learned that I had PD, three years after I got sober, I found that I had developed a strengthened union with my extraordinarily patient, loving wife. And in that year, 1994, Tracy became pregnant with twins, an extra baby to make up for lost time (or maybe a wink from God). People felt strangely comfortable asking if we were concerned about bearing more children while dealing with the open-ended escalation of a major neurological disorder, and the fear that the babies could inherit the disease. The question could be construed as inappropriate, but the answer was: We weren't concerned, nor should they be.

Doubling Down on Doubling Up

The twins were not playing nicely *in utero*. Tracy's labor was induced a month earlier than her due date because of a complication with the pregnancy. Twin-to-twin transfusion meant that one of the babies was dominating the food and blood supply, hogging the placenta, and gaining weight, while the other was gradually growing weaker. So we picked a date (thereby throwing the whole astrology thing into doubt). They were induced; and sure enough, Baby #1 debuted, pale and wan, weighing about four pounds, followed eight minutes later by Baby #2, closer to six pounds, fat and red as a tomato—and I swear, she was smiling. To this day (at twenty-five years of age), Baby #1, Aquinnah, beautiful, funny, and smart, not greedy or selfish, nevertheless is aware of what she needs and how to protect it. Of the two, she is the more independent and resolute. Baby #2, Schuyler, also beautiful—*they are twins*—is bright, generous, and always willing to share. At times, she is more concerned for others than for herself. I suspect she feels a modicum of guilt for being such a shitty womb-mate. Aquinnah has forgiven her sister for trying to kill her. We don't get involved. It's between the sisters.

However Parkinson's disease affected me during the early lives of Sam, Aquinnah, and Schuyler, they absorbed it as normal. And something good was happening in our family, because when it came to the decision to have yet another child, a fourth, we had no hesitation.

Tracy and I recall our conversation. The girls' fifth birthday party had wrapped up, and the guests had left. Exhausted, Tracy and I wallowed in the aftermath. Sipping a glass of wine while I nursed a Diet Coke, Tracy squinted at me and asked, "You know what I'm thinking?"

"If I knew what you were thinking, my life would be so much easier," I truthfully replied.

She laughed. "I just have this feeling like someone's not here yet."

I gestured around the room. "Well . . . the party's over. We're out of goodie bags."

Tracy clarified, sort of. "Our apartment isn't as noisy as it wants to be."

We did the math, and it all added up to Esmé.

For Esmé, Parkinson's has not only been a constant in her inner-family life, but she has been alive through the emergence and growth of The Michael J. Fox Foundation as a force in medical research. She sees my public persona as that of a civil activist, and a very available parent in semiretirement.

We couldn't have commissioned a more ideal child to be the last at home during the college diaspora years. One advantage gained by living with Esmé's spirit is that she has clearly, demonstrably, been here before. She reads and writes with a proficiency that reveals a nuanced understanding for a person her age. Still, she'll come to us for advice. I don't let on to her, but I am always humbled. She possesses an ease and facility with the strange and difficult, nothing throws her; no person, no place, no predicament, can discourage or distract her from her objective. We assumed Esmé would follow in her siblings' bootsteps and attend the same summer camp they had. Our youngest child, at age eight, kept her own counsel. She ruled out the camp the older kids attended, owing to the fact that she has peanut allergies, and her independent research uncovered that the old camp was not nut-aware. Scouring the internet, she personally initiated contact with a number of goober-intolerant camps, and with one in particular: Walt Whitman in New Hampshire, her favorite. So that's where she went. I bet she appreciates Walt Whitman, the poet and optimist, too. That's Esmé.

Time Travelers

Tracy and I have a theory about all of our kids; they are time machines. With cruel velocity, the energy of their very lives tumbles us forward in time— birth, grade school, friends, celebrations, crises real and perceived, social media, high school, college—until we're suddenly sitting in an empty house with rooms full of teddy bears; rock and roll posters; generations of game systems; clothes that you can't throw away but that won't be worn anymore; and girls' shoes, once jealously fought over, now ready for discard. I wish away my time while I wait for my children to come and visit. Only my wife is wise enough to realize that this is time for us; to slow it down, find our rhythm.

Strangely, I can relate Parkinson's to this; it's another way the disease has been a gift (albeit a gift that keeps on taking). The deliberation with which I approach each day, each second, each movement, each intention— can literally slow me down to a crawl. All of those seconds, all of those minutes, are considered; I have a mini-conversation with myself about my every move.

I'm taking my time. Time isn't taking me.

Empty Nest

Sam is more than thirty now. I don't know when or how it happened, but he is a fully functioning adult.

My work pertaining to him is essentially done. Because the woman I fell in love with—his mother—has superior genes, I fulfilled the Darwinian goal of any father, and co-created a taller, smarter, funnier, better-looking version of myself.

I did not finish high school with my class of '79 (GED class of '93), so I didn't know how to relate to my oldest child as he left for college. I had no experiences to share, no pithy advice about coeds; only cautionary tales from a few frat parties I crashed at UCLA during my early years as a starving actor in L.A. (Rule #1: Keep track of your beer cup.) It didn't seem real; no matter how many times I visited campuses with Sam and read over admission forms, I was still shocked when he actually left. I was also kind of pissed.

Sam and I share a special bond. Not just the stereotypical father/son stuff, and beyond the usual relationship that exists between a parent and their oldest child. Ours has always been a connection of shared interests and ideas: stomping through the woods in Vermont and Connecticut; our mutual love of rock music, from Frank Zappa to Led Zeppelin to Jay-Z; and the wide-ranging political conversations which have found him, surprisingly, even to the left of me.

Mostly, we share an appreciation of the absurd (I refer you back to politics and Frank Zappa).

Sam was my day-to-day guy, my buddy, my "ride or die" homie. And now he was gone. I knew it was just to college, but still, he was absent. We prepare our children to go off to school, and then they have the nerve to actually leave. They come home for a couple of days, get their laundry done, and spend more time with their friends from high school than they do with us. It's torture, really. We're proud, we're worried, concerned that they won't be able to get along without us—and then we're shattered when they do. We're left realizing that, as they begin to create their own future, we begin to face our own mortality.

———

As much as I love my wife and three daughters, after Sam headed to the West Coast, I was drowning in a sea of estrogen. I was feeling the need for a buddy that summer, when I read a notice on the bulletin board of the Chilmark General Store on Martha's Vineyard.

2

DOG YEARS

The term "rescue dog" brings two images to mind. One is semi-comic—the clichéd St. Bernard with a brandy cask dangling from his neck, looking for Alpine day-trippers lost in snowdrifts. The other one reverses the roles—I'm thinking of those devastating images from ASPCA ads with Sarah McLachlan and Eric McCormack, and those incredible folks who actually rescue dogs from excruciating pain and neglect. I admire them for their heartbreakingly difficult work. Otherwise, the use of the word "rescue," when applied to just doing something decent, like adopting a dog from a pound, or from a neighbor who is moving, strikes me as somewhat vainglorious. It just doesn't rise to the level of heroism. A reminder: we get something out of it, too. We get a dog, a friend, a confidante, and for me, another thing to trip over.

Growing up as an army brat, I never had a dog. Not that military service prohibits dog ownership; it's just that we moved around an awful lot, and to paraphrase an old axiom, "If the army wanted you to have a dog, they would've issued you one." As a young adult living on my own, I resumed a peripatetic lifestyle, frequently traveling for television and movie work. I did, however, welcome a few dogs into my life. Two dogs in particular stand out: One I met recently, close to home; the other crossed my path years ago, halfway around the world in Southeast Asia.

For much of the first part of 1988, I was in Thailand filming *Casualties of War*, a grueling, often lonely experience, even in the chaos of a film production. Tracy and I were engaged to be married soon after my return to the States, and I missed her on a cellular level. One day in April, on location in a village called Phang Nga, on the island of Phuket, I observed a family gathered by the beach. A small black-and-white puppy of indeterminable pedigree, a short rope leash dangling from his scruffy neck, romped around them. The family kept shooing him away. I'm a sucker for underdogs, literal and figurative. I crouched down and called him over. He bounced toward me as if he'd known me most of his life—which, at that point, he practically had. My driver, Wanchai, attempted to convince me that the puppy was not a pet, but protein, destined for a soup pot. Wanchai was probably taking the piss out of me, but it was true that the family didn't seem to be emotionally attached to the dog, at least in his current, non-entrée form. He wound up tagging along with me all day, and I decided that I wasn't going to leave him behind. I offered the family the Thai baht equivalent to ten American dollars, and they accepted.

It soon became obvious that my new friend was a pestilent mess. On my next day off, I brought him to a veterinarian on the island. After deworming, treating his mange, and riddling his body with a gamut of shots and vaccinations, the vet suggested I name him "Sanuk," a Thai word on the order of "peace" or "shalom;" an expression of goodwill, spiritual and emotional. I liked it. Sanuk stayed with me all through the spring and summer, right up to the point that we finally wrapped our marathon production and departed Thailand for home.

Sadly, there was no way I could subject Sanuk to the prohibitive quarantine process involved in exporting an animal from Asia to the United States. Two other dogs were living at the Amanpuri Resort in Phuket, my base during filming. Both belonged to the hotel's manager, and the hounds tolerated Sanuk as they would an exasperating kid brother. The little pup thrived there—why wouldn't he? Swimming pool, palm shade trees, and scraps from the kitchen. I appealed to the manager, who generously promised to take in Sanuk. Back in the U.S., I married Tracy, and every now and then I'd think about the little black-and-white puppy. She would have loved him.

A few years later, a friend mentioned that he had just vacationed at the Amanpuri in Thailand.

"I met your dog," he reported.

"You met my dog? A little black-and-white pup named Sanuk? Is he okay?"

"Yeah," he said. "He looks happy. Only they don't call him Sanuk. I guess they gave him a new name."

"What is it?"

"Michael J. Fox."

Gentle Giant

Gus was born in a shelter somewhere in the South. The litter of puppies was shuttled to another shelter in New England, where a very nice woman from Colorado adopted one of the males, and took him to her family's summer home on Martha's Vineyard. She soon discovered an allergy to dog hair. Through an oddly serendipitous series of events, I met Gus and brought him to my own home. Some may deem this a "rescue," but I don't. I didn't rescue Gus. You can argue that he rescued me, but he'd be too modest to make that claim. Gus and I just found each other. Lucky Gus, lucky me.

The Chilmark Store on Martha's Vineyard is a place to grab a slice of pizza or a cup of coffee, and settle on the porch. On any day in season, a cross-section of the hordes of summer people gather there to shop, snack, and chat, and maybe see one or two of the famous folks who spend time on the island. The person you're reaching across to grab a straw at the condiment counter could be Jake Gyllenhaal, or James Taylor, or Larry David—although he might smack your hand away. This is definitely where the cool people hang out. I tend to avoid it (not so much the store as the scene).

My friend Clark Gregg, along with his wife, Jennifer Grey, and their daughter, Stella, were vacationing with us. On the way home from playing golf, Clark suggested we pull into the Chilmark for a frozen coffee. I groaned. I wasn't in the mood to run across Alan Dershowitz holding court with his entourage, but it was a drippingly hot afternoon, and a frozen coffee held appeal. We emerged, coffeed up, and stepped onto the porch. On the store's weathered, shingle-clad wall, they have a bulletin board for people to post ads; babysitting services, guitar lessons, yard work, upcoming concerts, and community events. Through the clutter, a photograph caught my eye: a puppy up for adoption. The ad described him as a three-month-old, black-and-white Great Dane–Lab mix named "Astro," after the dog in the *Jetsons* cartoons. I didn't say anything or take the number down, but I had Astro on the brain.

That night at dinner, Tracy said to me: "I saw something interesting today on my bike ride. I stopped by the Chilmark Store, and there was an ad on the bulletin board . . ."

"For a dog? Astro?" I interrupted.

She put down her fork. "Yeah. Astro, the dog. How did you know?"

"You saw it too?" I asked. "We gotta meet this dog." And then I added, "I hope he doesn't have the name 'Astro' imprinted yet."

Four-Legged Son

Life with Gus (né Astro) is a revelation.

Late summer, 2008. I don't realize until Sam leaves and Gus shows up, that I have gradually been paring away at the physical side of my life. I can't run in a safe, reliable way anymore; my leaping and jumping are suspect; and I am a menace on the golf course. But I can still walk for days. Sam and I drifted away from doing anything much more physical than hiking, biking, and jumping in the pool. The latter, curiously, is the only thing Gus *won't* do. As much as he looks part retriever, his aversion to water clearly identifies him as a hound dog: lazy, but game for anything except the pool.

He has a similar negative reaction to the beach. He is restless, agitated, and has a psychotic break anytime Tracy or I, or one of the kids, disappear into the waves. Waiting desperately for us to emerge, he paces a trench in the sand, emits low, soft yelps, and searches frantically for someone to help. (*Anyone? Anyone?*) But he is not concerned enough to venture in himself. Eventually, we join him back on the beach, towel off, and try to talk him down. (I told you he's not a rescue dog.)

Once back in the city, our days begin early, with a 6:30 a.m. walk through Central Park. Still in shadows, the sun rising in the east, we patrol the horse trail surrounding the Reservoir. When we reach the turn at the power station, the path straightens out toward the halfway point. The sun begins to find us, and we quicken our steps. On the days when I can't make it to the park with Gus, the chore—though I wouldn't call it that—goes to a hired walker. The dog walkers in our neighborhood obviously work for the same company, and they're ubiquitous. About every other trip to the park, we run into a dog that Gus knows, and there'll be a good five to ten minutes of butt-sniffing, tail-wagging, mock aggression, and me listening to a dog walker chat about grad school.

For any dog lover, or simply any sentient human being, there is nothing quite like the energy of a puppy. It winds you up and wears you out at the same time. Still, Gus can get worn out and want to take a rest on the West Side. We'll do a lap around the Great Lawn, and then park ourselves on a bench for Gus to receive his admirers. Everyone loves this dog.

Tracy comments, "You know they're not stopping because of the dog; they're stopping to say hello to you."

"No, you don't get it. I'm invisible. All they see is forty pounds of four-month-old, black-and-white puppy, all ears and feet and tongue, and they fall in love instantly."

After a sufficient period of adulation, we wend our way across Central Park West at 81st Street to drop in at the Bull Moose Dog Run, on the north end of the Museum of Natural History. It is pure bedlam. Lots of dogs, lots of breeds, with lots of helicopter owners who should have calculated that bringing Precious to a dog park would likely result in encounters with other dogs. Gus, not through fault but by nature, is a madness-multiplier. His energy and conviviality bring him into contact with everybody, two legs or four. This is where I have to play my secreted liver treats wisely; I need to bribe him to get him out of there. Usually, a schnauzer or two comes around for a piece of the action. I shoo them away, wrestle the leash onto Gus's thick, meaty neck, and we are eastbound.

Gus and I have regular times and regular routes, both in the city and around our neighborhood on Long Island. In less than a year, he grows from forty pounds to one hundred and fifteen pounds. I don't have to bend an inch in order to rub his ears or scratch that spot between his eyes that he can't access. When I stop, he persistently head-butts my hand. He's so enormous now, our neighbors, city and country, comment on the sight of the two of us: a small man walking a horse. I'd give a desiccated liver treat for every time I've heard, "Why don't you get a saddle for that thing?"

Dog owners will recognize the relationship I'm describing. It's beyond owner-pet; it's an interspecies communion. I read somewhere, and have proved it through actual practice, that if you can maintain eye contact with an animal, especially a dog, for more than thirty seconds, a definite bond exists. Not to sound too creepy, but I can hold Gus's gaze for minutes on end. It's like he's awaiting instructions. He also responds to ridiculous verbal cues. "Gus," I'll suggest, "go grab your blanket." He'll bring me the brown one and I'll say, "No, no. The red one." And he'll respond by fetching the correct color.

There's a scene in *Once Upon a Time . . . in Hollywood*, one of my favorite films from one of my favorite directors, in which Brad Pitt returns home to his bull terrier, and lectures to him while opening and preparing cans of dog food. It's not what he says to his canine roommate that stands out to me; it's the recognition of the relationship, the intimacy and the respect that these two share. Spoiler alert: In the end, Brad's hero pit bull comes to the rescue and alters history.

I'll have to screen that scene for Gus sometime.

All of this is not to suggest that my relationship with Gus replaced or supplanted in some way my relationship with my son. There's obviously no sane way to compare the two. But the ache that I felt when Sam went away was eased and extenuated by the completely different role that a Great Dane–ish mutt now plays in my life. He keeps me moving, he keeps me present, and in an important way, he keeps me honest.

3

ACT TOO

As an actor, here's how I see myself: I can portray any human being, and some animals, as long as they have Parkinson's disease. My character on *Spin City*, Deputy Mayor Michael Flaherty, didn't have PD; so by the end of our second season, it was difficult for him to believably pass as physically uncompromised. Increasingly worried that my random movements would confuse the audience if they didn't know about my disease, and alienate them if they did (*Would they still think I'm funny if they knew I had PD?*), I chose to publicly disclose my condition in 1998. Indeed, the fans were accepting and supportive. But by 2000, after much deliberation, I made the decision to retire from the show and from show business. At age forty, my symptoms had advanced to a point I deemed career-ending.

In retrospect, I may have jumped the gun. My situation was evolving in unexpected ways. Whereas during my last season on *Spin City* I was tremoring and swaying with dyskinesias, the next couple of years of voluntary unemployment brought relief from some of the harsher PD symptoms. I found a movement disorder specialist, Dr. Susan Bressman, who completely reconfigured my pharmaceutical approach toward treating Parkinson's. She also put an emphasis on physical therapy, diet, and fitness. This period was restorative, less stressful, and allowed me to get a better grip on the disease.

Responsibilities with The Fox Foundation kept me constructively occupied during this time, and of course I had a dynamic family life with a wife and four school-aged kids. I was happy as a clam. But who wants to be a clam? I felt there was way too much *me* time. I wanted to be somebody else, at least for a few hours. After two years of retirement, the idea of acting again seemed more and more plausible—and maybe even necessary.

As if he had a direct line to my brain, my friend and *Spin City* co-creator, Bill Lawrence, called. He had a new show called *Scrubs*, a medical comedy set in a dysfunctional hospital, with a hysterical cast led by Zach Braff. Billy wanted to know if I felt up to doing an arc, a guest role that plays out over a few episodes. I was interested, although I had a few concerns. I issued a fair warning.

"I hate to be a diva, but you know I come with baggage. And when I say 'baggage,' I mean two rollies, a hat box, and a garment bag."

"And a fanny pack, I bet," Billy ventured. "What do you need? Longer breaks? Later call times?"

"All of that and more," I promised.

It was an interesting opportunity. The character Billy had in mind was Dr. Kevin Casey, an eccentric neurosurgeon with obsessive-compulsive disorder. The character was written with all of the classic OCD behaviors—handwashing, light switching, vocal tics—but I wouldn't focus on those. To me, they didn't represent the full person. I had to find Kevin's truth. It's not what a character reveals, it's what he's hiding that's intriguing.

I didn't have to search too deeply to find a point of connection with Dr. Kevin Casey. He met me where I was.

J.D. CONFRONTS DR. CASEY IN THE SURGICAL SCRUB AREA, WHERE HE IS WASHING HIS HANDS.

J.D.
(forcefully)
Kevin, I have to talk to you. Right now.

THIS INTERRUPTS CASEY'S THOROUGH HAND CLEANING. HE SHUTS OFF THE FAUCET WITH HIS ELBOW AND TURNS ON J.D.

DR. CASEY
Damn it!

J.D.
(suddenly losing his bravado)
Later's cool, too.

DR. CASEY
I spent the last few days meeting new people and trying to get used to this place. I'm stressed and I'm fried, and I just wanna go home. But here's the punchline. Even though my last surgery was two hours ago, I can't stop washing my damn hands.

CASEY SCREAMS WITH FRUSTRATION AND THROWS THE SOAP ACROSS THE ROOM.

J.D.
I'm sorry.

DR. CASEY

No, I'm sorry. I'm sorry. This is a weak moment.
Nobody's supposed to see this.

HE TAKES A BEAT.

I'll clean up the soap. Probably several thousand times.
Everyone's got their own burdens, J.D. And I'm not going to be
one of those people who dumps mine on somebody else.
Now, what do you need?

J.D.

Nothing.

J.D. STUDIES DR. CASEY. THE SCENE DISSOLVES INTO MONTAGE:
DR. CASEY GOING THROUGH HIS END-OF-THE-DAY RITUALS.
COLDPLAY'S "EVERYTHING'S NOT LOST" ACCOMPANIES.

J.D.

(interior voiceover)
I think owning your burdens is half the battle.
Still, it's not that daunting if you look around and see
what other people have to deal with.

My two episodes on *Scrubs* provided a test, of sorts, and in my humble opinion, I think I passed. I didn't present the audience with a character who had Parkinson's disease, but one with OCD.

I discovered I could focus less on the externals and stop trying to hide my symptoms. This was in stark relief from my days on *Spin City*, when I'd keep a live audience waiting while I paced my dressing room, pounding my arm with my fist in a vain attempt to quell the tremors. On *Scrubs*, instead of trying to kill it, I invited Parkinson's with me to the set.

I felt free to concentrate on what any actor, able-bodied or not, is charged with accomplishing: uncovering the internal life of another human being. Putting the emphasis on my character's vulnerabilities and not my own, Parkinson's could in fact disappear, and be morphed into whatever my character was living with. My inability to still my hands echoed Dr. Casey's inability to cease scrubbing his own. As for his vocal tics and repetitions, I could find a version of that pattern from my own experience. And the slower pace in my stride transformed into his hesitation when walking into new environments. It became about who he was, and not what he had.

Moreover, not what I had.

I began thinking more broadly about what possibilities my future could hold. Suddenly, I was open for business again. Instead of allowing my idiopathy to deter me from employment, I created a new blueprint for myself: how to be a working actor with a disability. I'd co-opt the disease, get PD to do a little acting of its own, and bring my Parkinson's into the family business.

There had been previous inquiries about my willingness and availability to work, and other guest role offers, before Bill Lawrence reached out. Not wanting to set myself up for failure, I had demurred. But I gained a lot from those two weeks on *Scrubs*. I realized that we all have our burdens. Every character has a bear inside that they're wrestling with, no matter where they are and what they're doing. As an actor, I suddenly wanted more opportunities to take on that bear.

So, yes. I was right. I *can* play anyone, as long as they have Parkinson's. And as I was discovering, *everyone has Parkinson's*.

Please Come to Boston

I am billionaire businessman Daniel Post, on a date with attorney Denise Bauer (Julie Bowen). Flirting, laughing, we discuss the evening's further possibilities. It's a sexy scene, and things will only heat up from here. We're filming a night location shoot for *Boston Legal*, a well-crafted legal drama infused with David E. Kelley's wry sense of humor. Julie Bowen's brilliance and generosity as an actor makes me feel secure, yet keeps me on my toes.

Daniel Post has stage-four cancer. *Enter from the shadows: the bear.* Daniel's billions are of no use to him. The writers masterfully set up the conflict of a doomed man with more fortune than future. They also include scenes where I am required to be romantically intimate. I only mention this because of the physical confidence it takes to perform these scenes, in particular. I don't want to wrap my arms around the leading lady and shake her like a martini.

For me professionally, *Boston Legal* was an ideal follow-up to *Scrubs*. After we wrap production, what I remember most from that first night is the smell of carbon in the air, emanating from the arc, the huge moveable klieg light that illuminated the sidewalk. It smelled like show business. I was working, and I loved it.

It all combined to set me up for an Emmy nomination, a nice surprise, and a great honor.

—

The next decade-plus would play out in unexpected and deeply gratifying ways. Keeping an active schedule, I applied myself to the work of The Fox Foundation. It amazed me what we'd been able to accomplish in a short amount of time. Our team created a forceful presence in philanthropic research, and the organization quickly grew to serve the needs of many—patients, families, and the scientists we fund. During this period, I also wrote a few books, and somehow nurtured the second act of my career.

Each acting offer came with the opportunity to play an interesting character. That was the cool thing: They were *characters*. Somewhere, somehow, between *Spin City* and *Boston Legal*, I had become a character actor. I can think of no higher calling for a thespian. Some of my all-time favorite supporting performers include Edward G. Robinson, Thelma Ritter, Strother Martin, Jack Warden, and a contemporary I've worked with, John C. Reilly. When I first moved to L.A. and joined the Screen Actors Guild, I changed my professional name as a nod to another favorite character actor, Michael J. Pollard.

There's a consistency in the best work of Pollard and these others; a fluidity and integrity. Free of the onus of carrying the story, they can explore the idiosyncratic and even the extreme.

I didn't miss being the leading man. I think of that Hollywood truism that explains the difference between a short actor and a short movie star: to appear taller in a shot, a short actor stands on a box, while a short movie star makes everyone else stand in a ditch. I had discovered the simple pleasures of the ditch, where vanity has no value.

Tommy, Denis, Dwight, & Me

Another old friend with a wire to my brain—actor, writer, producer Denis Leary—is one of the great wildcards in my life, and one of the most creative and prolific writers I know. So, when he called with an offer to do a few episodes of his hit series *Rescue Me*, I was listening.

"Fox, you've got to do my show."

"Keep talking," I said. "Who's the guy?"

"Dwight. The boyfriend of my ex-wife," Denis said. "He's nuts. A bitter, angry, lonely, pill-popping, alcoholic, sarcastic, sex-addicted shit-head. And, oh . . ." he added, "he's a paraplegic."

This was a lot to take in.

"Uh, Denis," I asked, "what part of this guy made you sit up and say, *Let's call Mike Fox?* Never mind all the other stuff, how am I supposed to play paralyzed? You understand that I can't stop moving? This guy's in a wheelchair, and I'm a human whirligig."

"Yeah," Denis said. "You'll figure it out."

One of my favorite scenes out of my five *Rescue Me* episodes estab-lished the animosity between Dwight and Denis's character, Tommy. Mid-argument, with his wheelchair folded and leaning against the wall, inaccessible, Dwight throws himself from the couch to the floor and commando-crawls toward Tommy, who retreats as Dwight howls epithets. In the aftermath of the fracas, Dwight cracks a vulgar joke to himself, fol-lowed by a rueful laugh as he exults in the chaos. Somehow a fragile truce is established between the two, and Dwight invites Tommy to go for a ride in his super-charged, convertible muscle car, with hand-controlled throt-tle, brake, clutch, and gearshift. The other element of some importance: Dwight is high on pills, sopping drunk, and whenever he inexplicably has a free hand, he chug-a-lugs from the beer can wedged between his seat and the console, all the while bragging about his sexual prowess with Tom-my's ex-wife. A wild ride; even the film crew was terrified. *Alex Keaton, we hardly knew ye.*

It was one of my favorite roles of my career, and this time, I won the Emmy. Thanks, *Rescue Me*. Thanks, Denis.

It's Personal

Larry David had an idea that, not surprisingly, sounded hysterically funny, totally irreverent, and potentially offensive. I knew that *Curb Your Enthu-*

siasm was largely improvised, with narrative objectives established by the writers and producers, and prompts to help performers advance the plotline. So instead of sending me a script, Larry pitched me the story:

"I move to New York," he said, "to get out of this charity thing in Los Angeles. And one night at a restaurant, I see you, *Michael J. Fox, you*, and a couple of friends, having a drink. I kind of give a 'hello' hand signal, and you shake me off."

"I shake you off? How do I do that?" I ask.

"With your head. The way you move your head seems judgmental."

"Wait, you think I'm judging you with my head?"

"Yeah, I'm offended by the way you shake your head, in judgment."

"You know that's the Parkinson's."

"Yeah, well, I take it personally."

I have to laugh. "Nice."

Larry continued with what was becoming the most ridiculously funny pitch, ever.

"Then, one night I'm in my new apartment, and my upstairs neighbor is really annoying, stomping around and making a lot of noise, so I go upstairs to confront him, and I find out it's you. Now I'm convinced that you're faking Parkinson's, just to piss me off. I lean in and give you 'the big eyeball'—the look I give to people I don't trust."

I giggle. "I love the eyeball."

"So, you invite me in, try to calm me down. I watch you. I know I'm going to catch you at something. You offer me a drink and grab a Diet Coke from the fridge. All the way to the table, your hand is shaking, so when I open the soda, it explodes in my face. And the feud escalates from there."

What Larry was suggesting really pushed it to the edge. I suppose it could've been a disaster, if people—especially PD patients and their families—mistook my openness for self-ridicule. But I saw it as liberating. After all those years of hiding my symptoms, sometimes overmedicating to achieve and maintain kinetic neutrality, I could let it go. After Larry's pitch, I not only wanted to be in the show, I couldn't wait to watch it.

The Good Ride

I follow Tracy's footprints in the sand from the shore break until I reach her on the towel where she sits, glistening in the sun and wringing the seawater out of her hair. I collapse into a wooden canvas beach chair, an instrument of torture, and try to get comfortable. This is when the lady approaches. I don't know her. I haven't seen her on the beach before.

"Mr. Fox?" she says, looking me in the eye with a seriousness that seems incongruous with the setting. "I have to make a confession to you."

Not exactly the words you want to hear from a stranger. Now she had Tracy's attention, too.

"Watching you walk down to the water with your wife, I got this feeling of revulsion, hatred, and loathing. I couldn't figure out why. And then I realized, you're Louis Canning. You are despicable."

I laugh and say, "Oh, I'm flattered."

Louis Canning definitely made an impression. This was the big surprise of my post-career career; the guest role on *The Good Wife* that turned into a twenty-six-episode run over four seasons. The writer/producers, Robert and Michelle King, called to offer me a short arc during the show's sophomore season—the part of a lawyer, disabled and wheelchair-bound. Coming off of *Rescue Me*, I didn't think it was a good idea to repeat myself. So, we compromised.

Tardive dyskinesia, a disorder featuring symptoms in common with Parkinson's, is the disability we bestowed upon Louis Canning, equity partner and lead litigator in the firm Canning & Meyers. Louis tremored less than if he had Parkinson's, but he had similar problems with balance, gait, and sometimes speech. A sort of large-motor, slow-motion spasticity, not ideal for a high-powered litigator.

Within weeks, I am working on a courtroom set, in a makeshift studio in Brooklyn. My character introduces himself to a group of prospective jurors during the voir dire process of jury selection.

LOUIS

Before I ask you just a few questions, I probably owe you an explanation. This movement you see. This. You probably noticed that, huh?

SOME CHUCKLES, LAUGHS. HE STUDIES THE JURORS, WALKING UP AND DOWN THE LINE, SEEING WHO MEETS HIS EYE, WHO DOESN'T.

LOUIS (continued)

I suffer from tardive dyskinesia. That's a funny word for a neurological syndrome. It makes me do this . . .
(making fun of himself)
Aghhha-aghhhhha.

MORE CHUCKLES.

LOUIS (continued)

If you just look at me long enough, you'll get used to it.
Go ahead, look. I don't mind.

Louis goes on to tell the jury that when his symptoms worsen, he relies on medication, a vial of which he conveniently produces from his breast pocket and waves before the potential jurors. The case he's about to defend is on behalf of a pharmaceutical company, accused of manufacturing tainted pills.

Unlike *Rescue Me*'s Dwight, who soaks in his misery, the *Good Wife* writers created a character who shamelessly exploits his own misfortune, converting it into an asset to win sympathy and jury votes. This was twisted fun for me on two levels: I got to play a guy who took the worst part of his life and turned it into the best part of his work. He used his disability to extract empathy and good will in pursuit of victory. Level two: Disabled and differently abled characters are always seen in a sympathetic light, soft piano music rising to crescendo as they achieve their relatively modest goals. This guy was different. He was debilitated, but no piano.

He was an asshole.

It's easy to dismiss Louis Canning as a manipulative jerk, but he's more complicated than that. He exploits his handicap to induce sympathy and good will with jurors, which on its face is unethical and inappropriate. But I think there's something else in play. I know from experience that people have an aversion to anyone who moves differently. Louis Canning succeeded in preempting that reaction by projecting a friendly and forthcoming demeanor. With the writing on the show so good, and Louis so well conceived, even Parkinson's couldn't screw it up.

One of my reasons for leaving *Spin City* was that I felt my face was no longer as expressive as I needed it to be. I had always liked being an actor that editors would cut to at any time for an appropriate reaction, my face always alive in a scene. Whether speaking or not, my character would be animated and engaged. Gradually, with the effects of Parkinson's, my face began retreating to a passive, almost frozen disposition. It was blank, and I was hard-pressed to enliven it in any way that didn't seem artificial.

Acting is what I do, and I needed to find a new way to do it. Instead of focusing on the notes I could no longer hit, I'd focus on my new instrument. It's not an electric, it's acoustic. It's not a Les Paul, it's a Hummingbird. Ultimately, I found that the philosophy of "less is more" works for me, which is convenient, because I have less. But as I'd discover, there's more to less than I thought.

Louis Canning taught me that I could utilize my blank expression and employ it as his inscrutable, enigmatic persona. My absence became his attitude; my deficit, his asset.

The array of characters I embodied in my second career all had something in common: all were over-achievers (Dwight was no exception); all were passionate; all had a flaw that was relatable to my own. Each had a vulnerability, and a corresponding point of damage. Add a dash of humor to that pathos, and I'd done a day's work.

Forgive the mention, but these shows, post-retirement, led me to eight Emmy nominations. Actually, it was nine: one more as a producer with my partner, Nelle Fortenberry, for a documentary we filmed in Central Asia—every bit as remarkable a journey as the professional one I was in the midst of experiencing.

4

HIGH TIMES

After a long flight to Frankfurt and a seven-hour layover in Delhi, we make a quick stop in Kathmandu, Nepal, to drop off and pick up passengers. I'm hearing Bob Seger's "Katmandu" on my inner iPod as we gain altitude. Stunning vistas beguile me, and soon the view will be supersized. Apparently not bound by post-9/11 FAA standards, the Drukair pilots invite me to join them in the cockpit for the last leg of the trip. They strap me into a jump seat, and continue the climb into the thin blue ether. I fall into a silent reverie at the majesty of Mt. Everest out the cockpit window, but the pilots want to talk movies and television, thrilled to have Marty McFly peering over their shoulders for the hour-long flight. Though I am happy to indulge my hosts, I worry that my showbiz small talk will distract this pair of twentysomething aviators. (I'd learn later that the facts flew—literally—in the face of my ageism. These guys are expert pilots, part of a small, elite group who are specifically trained and certified to land at the airport in Paro.)

Flying over the Himalayas is like housesitting for God . . . until our sudden close encounter with a massive white wall of death; the sheer, icy edifice of a Himalayan peak. A last-minute, ninety-degree right turn kicks up a swirl of glacial crystals, and we execute a precipitous, gut-wrenching dive to an abbreviated runway. The young pilot is as calm as a soccer mom driving a minivan through a Walmart parking lot. After a shockingly abrupt but smooth landing, we are safe. We have touched down in the mysterious, miraculous Kingdom of Bhutan. Some call it Shangri-la. While Bhutan, the country and its people, welcome us, they do require that we jump through hoops and sideswipe a few mountains in order to be their guests. Hey, if it was easy, everybody would be here.

It's the spring of 2009. My producing partner Nelle Fortenberry and I, along with our small documentary film crew, have flown to the top of the world to film a network television special. Nelle and I have worked together since the first season of *Spin City*. Talented and unflappable as she is, the challenge of this project doesn't intimidate her or dampen her appreciation for this journey. Nelle's expertise, along with that of our other executive producer, Rudy Bednar, assures that the work will be done. Also part of the team is my steadfast assistant, Nina Tringali. Trustworthy in any situation, she is smart, intuitive, and vigilant; at five foot ten, she literally watches over me.

The project serves as a documentary companion to my second book, *Always Looking Up*, adopting its subtitle, *Adventures of an Incurable Optimist*, as the name of the program. We conceived it as an exploration of the power of optimism in my life and elsewhere. Through supplemental investigations, more curious than scientific, we spotlight those whose optimistic worldview has positively affected others—from an average New Yorker who doles out newspapers and a gleeful affirmation each morning at an Upper West Side subway station; to musicians who offer uplifting lyrics; to sports stars who don't let defeat defeat them; to the Chicago Cubs, at the time still amid a one-hundred-year drought keeping them from a World

Series title, but whose players and loyal fans continue to believe in the promise of each new season.

Which brings us to the Kingdom of Bhutan. You've never heard of it? You are not alone. This small nation is located at the eastern end of the Himalayas in South Asia. It is bordered to the east and south by India; to the north by the Tibet Autonomous Region of the People's Republic of China; and to the west, it is separated from Nepal by the Indian state of Sikkim. Agriculture, forestry, and tourism are the pillars of Bhutan's economy. Its major source of revenue is the sale of hydroelectric power to India.

Relatively few tourists are adventurous enough to visit Bhutan, but those who do appreciate the handicrafts, weaving, and religious art that its people produce. There is a daily fee for each visitor, as much as five hundred dollars per day, and mandatory accompaniment by a government assigned guide. The Kingdom has no railroads. A challenging landscape that varies from hilly to ruggedly mountainous has made the building of roads and other infrastructure difficult and expensive.

They definitely saved money on airport runways.

If You're Happy and You Know It . . .

Bhutan's forbidding topography and landlocked status hinders the country's trade with other nations—not that Bhutan regards trade in traditional terms. While it does measure its GNP (Gross National Product), it is the GNH (Gross National *Happiness*) that is of greater importance to its people, government, and king. Bhutan is the only country known to measure happiness by this metric. Key to this concept, its Parliament is determined to preserve the nation's traditional culture and identity, and to avoid destruction of the environment. Accordingly, Bhutan has been rated "the happiest country in Asia," and is a perennial contender for the happiest country in the world, according to a global survey conducted by the University of Leicester. When the government lifted a ban on television and the internet in 1999, Bhutan became one of the last countries to introduce television. (This was the same year I retired from *Spin City*. Coincidence?) In weighing isolation versus careful progress, the king chose to lead the people toward the future, citing in his proclamation speech, "Television is a critical step to the modernization of Bhutan, as well as a major contributor to the country's Gross National Happiness." Personally, I saw very little Bhutanese television, just snippets of CNN International in the hotel room. I don't think they are bingeing.

A kingdom of fiercely loyal and loving subjects, the people voiced rare opposition to King Jigme Singye Wangchuck when he established a constitutional democracy over the traditional one-person rule. People accepted it, but still behaved as if Bhutan was a pure monarchy. In 2006, he abdicated the throne peacefully and lovingly to his son, Jigme Khesar Namgyel Wangchuck, who commands the same reverential regard from the people, despite his young age. Just twenty-five when he ascended to the throne, he became the youngest reigning monarch and head of state of the world's newest democracy. Almost to a person, every Bhutanese man or woman that I meet refers to him reverentially as "my king."

———

At the airport in Paro, if the Customs and Immigration officers are Grossly Happy, it's not evident. They are taciturn, efficient, and brusque. Having offered satisfactory answers to their questions, we are allowed to proceed to the baggage area and then out to our waiting cars, where our drivers are as happy as advertised. They take us from Paro, the flattest part of the country (hence the placement of the airport), to the capital city of Thimphu, along a route that traces the bends and turns of the Paro River Valley. Much of the country remains inaccessible for those without a specific purpose and extraordinary determination to get from point A to point B.

At first glance, the Paro area had impressed me as rustic and rugged, whereas our arrival in Thimphu finds us in a charming Asian mini-metropolis. Almost all of its citizenry adhere to a dress code—women in traditional *kiras*, long aprons covered by fashionable jackets called *tegos*, and men in knee-length robes or *ghos*. For official business, their outfits are adorned by scarves differentiated in color and style to signify rank and affiliation.

Like its populace, each building in Thimphu, every bit of signage, is an expression of the nation's culture. In the town's main intersection, where one might expect to see a traffic signal, there is a uniformed officer ensconced in a tremendously ornate kiosk, orchestrating the flow of humans and vehicles. Thimphu is the only capital city in the world without a single traffic light.

We check into our hotel, which surprisingly features all of the mod cons. The rooms are spacious and the food tasty. My only complaint would be the number of dogs, incessantly barking as they wander the streets around the hotel. Are they *happy* barks? I can't tell.

Whoever let the dogs out, eventually lets them back in. Everyone in our group reports a good night's sleep, important because we have a busy day of filming ahead. First off, we aim to get a handle on what the Bhutanese are talking about when they reference GNH. Since we are in the nation's seat of government, we're able to gain rare access to the impressive array of Parliament buildings. For our documentary, I interview Dasho Karma Tshiteem, formerly the Secretary of Bhutan's Planning Commission. This state organization was recently rebranded, giving Mr. Tshiteem the grand title "Secretary of Gross National Happiness." This nomenclature is the king's way of prodding government planners to apply the principles of GNH to Bhutan's economic challenges.

Mr. Tshiteem's job is to figure out how to boost morale as this long-isolated country hurtles toward modernization. He says that the concept of GNH has forced him to think more broadly about what adds to and subtracts from a person's well-being—and how that affects the national mood. "Trust in government is important, leisure time is important. For psychological well-being to flourish, all the other domains are important."

He notes that, "Once you cross a certain threshold, money doesn't get you more happiness. Our main concern is that if you have growth which is blind, fed by people's growing consumption, it's not really sustainable. What we are trying to do in our own little context is see what pattern of growth will be sustainable and desirable."

Fellow Traveler

The secretary introduces me to another government minister, a fortyish gentleman who has been diagnosed with Parkinson's disease. Not part of the official agenda, this is a casual meeting in a small room off the main corridor, away from the cameras. This quiet, thoughtful man, elegant in his *gho*, obviously weighed discretion against the opportunity to speak to me on a patient-to-patient basis. His symptoms are not especially dramatic, but feature a left-hand tremor and a subtle slowness of speech and movement, or bradykinesia. Apparently, his progression to this point has been fairly steady.

We talk about medication and treatment in our respective countries. He discloses that even in his position, he has limited access to PD drugs beyond the basic levodopa. Then, as often happens when speaking with fellow Parkinson's patients, the conversation relaxes into a give-and-take about our real-life stories. He has disclosed his condition to only a trusted few. He is as concerned about his future as would be any newly diagnosed Parkinson's patient. I lived in that state of trepidation and isolation for the first years of my own life with PD. And here on the far side of the planet, this gentleman expresses the same experience. Disease has a way of connecting us.

Moreover, we have another malady in common: golf. The minister points out that Bhutan is especially proud of their one golf course, and he encourages me to at least go to the driving range. Due to the elevation in the Himalayas and the thinness of the air, the ball travels extraordinary distances. Alas, I haven't the time, though it would be a radical improvement to my game. If not my long drives, then surely my putting would be a little steadier.

Stirred but Not Shaking

Something unexpected and magical has developed since I arrived in Bhutan: my Parkinson's symptoms have lessened to the point where they are barely noticeable, not only to others, but to my own inner gyroscope. I have to remind myself to take my meds. As there is little need, I take less than prescribed. Surprisingly, it has taken me a full day to acknowledge what is happening. I keep quiet about my observations at first, and when speaking with the minister, I choose discretion. What is happening for me is not happening for him. This is intriguing. Is it emotional? Chemical? Is it spiritual, a period of grace? Parkies are notoriously prone to placebo effects . . . If that's what this is, then toss me another sugar pill. I feel renewed. Could it be a reaction to the altitude (we are above 7,600 feet), or the interaction of the altitude sickness meds with my own? Or is it just the very palpable sense of contentment, ease, and Zenned-out bliss?

Although I'm not a Buddhist or subscriber to any particular orthodoxy, while in Bhutan I happily and respectfully observe a number of Buddhist conventions and rituals, such as spinning prayer wheels and maintaining meditative silence while visiting temples and shrines. You'd expect that adhering to these unfamiliar codes would seem awkward and perfunctory, but it doesn't. My behavior simply acknowledges that I am in an entirely different place, having a unique experience, and possibly transforming and changing on a molecular level.

I can't believe how "normal" I feel, given how abnormal the moment. The decrease in symptoms—tremor, bradykinesia, and Parkinsonian gait—is a puzzle. When I'm back in the States under ordinary circumstances, my symptoms don't come on suddenly. I'll be feeling fine, and then the meds will begin to wear off. There are a subtle series of tics, aches, and tremors; physical clues that tell me when it's time for another round of pharmaceuticals. I ignore them at my peril; when symptoms arrive, they punish my inattention. But not so up here in the mountain kingdom. What mild warnings I receive never seem to fully develop. Rather than jump up and down with glee, I simply accept it, with gratitude. I medicate perfunctorily, just so my body doesn't react negatively to a deficit, but it hardly seems necessary.

Having Parkinson's is being in constant flux; in and out, on and off. Every reaction to the drugs is met with an equal and opposite reaction when they wear off. So you're constantly trying to keep your foot on the cat's tail until your toe starts tapping—and then the cat gets loose, and you have to chase it down all over again. That feeling is absent in Bhutan; there is no "on" and "off."

Postcard from Punakha

We leave Thimphu early the next morning, a low mist hanging over the surrounding hills, our vehicles trailed for a while by the ubiquitous yapping dogs. During one day's travel from the capital city of Thimphu to the Punakha Valley, we'll traverse three temperate zones. We slog through mud on switchback roads, commercial trucks passing with mere inches of sloppy red dirt between safety and a three-hundred-foot drop to the valley floor. I remember monologist Spalding Gray's admonition based on his time in Indonesia: *Never drive in a country that believes in reincarnation.*

With the cool heights of Thimphu behind us, we follow the National Highway as it climbs through pine and hemlock forest. It crosses over the Dochula Pass at 10,300 feet, and then quickly descends into the lush and fertile Punakha Valley. What I see overwhelms me; it's so beautiful as to be impossible. Every turn of the head presents a new tableau, as basic as a splash of watercolor on a piece of parchment; as complex as the patterns in a peacock's tail feathers. One such vista includes not peacocks but cranes, flying low in loose formation over the surface of a tumbling river, across which a farmer drives his team of riding ponies. The landscape exists to be painted by a master.

But wait, it gets better. In a low grassy field, approximately one hundred yards apart, two groups of traditionally clad archers let loose a volley of arrows in a high parabola. After reaching their apex, the darts rocket down to their targets. Adding drama to their competition, one or two members of the receiving team always seem to be directly in the path of the incoming projectiles. They step spryly out of the way before instructing their archers to return fire. Laughter and Punakhan smack talk rings through the lush valley. It's a scene both exotic and as familiar to me as an old *Wide World of Sports* episode.

Most of the river valley is dedicated to rice paddies. Now and then in the distance, a house and outbuildings overlook the terraces. Odd but attractive conflations of pagoda and alpine chalet, the structures are rustic but well built. It must be reported that almost every home is conspicuously adorned with a larger-than-life–sized painting of a phallus—sometimes more than one. A cluster of three, arranged like flowers, creates a sort of bouquet of boners. The consensus seems to be that they bring good luck. No one can tell us with certainty when all of this penis portraiture became part of life in Bhutan, but the oldest structure that sports a phallus is a fifteenth-century monastery. Today, these paintings adorn residences and businesses, and even some schools and restaurants.

Invited inside one of these homes, Nelle, the crew, and I fit comfortably into the surprisingly large, wood-paneled central room, furnished with a number of pillows on the floor surrounding a wood stove. The farmer, his wife, and their children offer us a traditional lunch of chilies and cheese with red rice, served at a low table that we all gather around. The language barrier is deep and wide, but with our guides translating, we manage to share thoughts, ideas, and even humor. Like most farmers in Bhutan, they express great satisfaction in their labor, and pride in the result.

Aside from the beautiful, sun-warmed faces of our host family, my fondest memory of the meal is the sweet taste of warm goat's milk, offered to me by the family matriarch.

After bidding goodbye to our hosts and presenting them with gifts of betel nut leaves and beer, I take a short walk down to the rice paddies. Keeping my eyes peeled for cobras, I dance along the ridge rows. I have been in Bhutan for three days. My fellow travelers may have picked up on this new kick in my step, but I'm not talking about it. I feel like if I acknowledge it, I'll chase it away. *Move along, Mike; nothing to see here.* I already sense its impermanence; I'm not cured, but I feel no less grateful. No jump-from the-wheelchair-toss-the-crutches-aside, *It's a miracle!* moment. It isn't like that. Just a few moments of grace that seem to be spilling over into days.

The following morning, we hurry to our next location, where I will sit still for hours (an impossible feat under normal circumstances), cross-legged (beyond impossible), amid monks and thousands of Bhutanese. We are attending the Punakha Festival, a religious and cultural gathering at the intersection of the rivers Pho Chhu and Mo Chhu. Our guide, Tshewang, accompanies me to the center of the vortex. The riot of color and costume, incense and intensity, unfolds in the courtyard of the colossal Punakha Dzong, a massive stone fortress that previously served as Bhutan's administrative capitol. The crowd makes way for warriors who dance among us, reenacting the four-hundred-year-old Bhutanese victory over Tibet. Drummers pound and dancers weave and sway as the clamor and clang of the celebration dissolves in the ear like a hum. A young monk, swathed in a crimson robe, offers me a fallen leaf from the courtyard's bodhi tree. He clasps his hands, closes his eyes, and nods gently. What would it be like to live a life like this?

A Nest Too Far

We spend our last full day of filming back in Paro. Our plan is to visit Tiger's Nest, a seventeenth-century Buddhist monastery clinging to a cliffside in the Upper Paro Valley. Most of our group won't make it all the way to the sacred temple, but we'll still have a rigorous hike to Taktsang Cafeteria, a teahouse at the halfway point. During our pre-production meetings in New York, it was assumed that, given my health issues, the ruggedness of the trail, and the six-hour round-trip journey, I would sit out this portion of the shoot, and later provide narration to the footage our crew would collect. There is surprise, and some concern, when I announce the night before the hike that I am going to take part. I inform Rudy and Nelle that I will go with them as far as the teahouse—but this is still no walk in the park.

Our vehicles commandeer the parking lot at the base of the trail and disgorge producers, crew, Bhutanese guides, Nina, and me. We hit the trail, a winding cart-path and a hell of a steep trek. We come across a young Bhutanese girl, around eight or nine years old, selling trinkets and betel nut leaves. My guide, Tshewang, communicates to her that we can't stop to shop now. She smiles, lets us pass, and then by her own secret route, scampers ahead and is waiting trailside when we round the next switchback, to make another sales pitch. Amazed that it is the same girl, and wholly impressed by her initiative, I purchase a little wooden box from her to put my bodhi leaf in. She shows up three switchbacks later, just to say thank you.

We reach the teahouse, gulping for air and gawking at the vista. Taking advantage of this stunning background, we shoot some b-roll footage and set up for a couple of quick interviews.

Rudy points the camera at me and tosses out a few simple questions: "So what do you think? Are these the happiest people on earth?"

I answer, "They don't claim to be. Sure, the people of Bhutan are friendly, engaging, and yes, happy and welcoming. But the contention was never that they were the happiest people on earth, but that they had found a formula for measuring and nurturing happiness. What makes Gross National Happiness more than just a silly government policy is the earnestness of the population to cooperate and participate in the things that make life richer, and not just from an economic perspective."

"And you?" Rudy queries. "How are you doing?" With a smile, I describe the relief from Parkinson's symptoms I've been experiencing since arriving in the country. I can't explain it and I don't need to, as my physical presence—steady and spasm-free—says it all. As for my state of mind, I give an account of feeling grateful. Unable to fully understand the renewal and wellness I'm currently enjoying, I simply welcome it and surf the wave.

I look over my shoulder at Tiger's Nest. At that moment, I decide that I'm going to climb as high as I can today.

We chug the last of our tea and pack extra water. I transfer the bodhi leaf from my wallet into the small wooden box, and hand it to Nina for safekeeping. Normally, I would take it for luck, but I already feel plenty lucky.

After some demanding and inhospitable terrain, we're able to get a closer view of Tiger's Nest. There's still a great distance to go, but it's a more captivating perspective than from the teahouse. Melded into the jagged cliff face, as if by sheer force of will, is the temple. Its white, pagoda-like segments, perched upon a series of red rooftops, bring to mind a layered wedding cake. Thousands of prayer flags dance in the breeze. The belief is that this is the place Guru Padmasambhava arrived on a flying tigress in the eighth century, meditating in the caves for three years before emerging to bring Buddhism to Bhutan. I would welcome a ride if the tigress shows up, because I don't know how much farther I can go.

Satisfied with my effort, I inform Tshewang that this is far enough for me. With that, I spit on my palm, grip my walking stick, and go back down to the teahouse in half the time it took us to climb up. Now on the switchback part of the trail, I find myself struggling to maintain a measured pace. The loose scree, marbles of gravel beneath my boots, causes me to travel faster than I intend. Ironically, this is similar to a Parkinsonian problem called "festination," literally "to act or move at high speed." This is when our footfall increases at a faster rate than our bodies can maintain; our stride shortens, and we find ourselves feet together, up on our toes, starting to pitch forward.

It occurs to me that I am about to do an ugly face-plant, with momentum. Quick decision: Tamp the velocity of falling forward and down by throwing myself sideways. In doing this, I take a shortcut thirty feet through the brush to the next switchback. The incident costs me a pound of flesh and a case of Himalayan road rash. At least I don't take out any young Bhutanese entrepreneurs.

The stuntman in me is chagrined that half of our camera crew is still climbing to Tiger's Nest, while the others are waiting down at the trailhead. No one was there to capture on video my heroic forward shoulder roll. Along with my intrepid guide, Nelle and Nina are the first on the scene. They find my wipe-out horrifying, until they see that I'm okay, and then they find it hilarious. As for Tshewang, he miraculously produces a first aid kit from inside his *gho* and is already swabbing the cuts and scrapes with alcohol. He wipes the bloody scratches and picks out the pebbles embedded in the palms of my hands. Tshewang looks worried, either about me or his job security. I like to think it is the former. I notice that one of the fingers on my left hand seems a little wonky, but it doesn't hurt.

Color My World

That evening, our last night in Bhutan, we have dinner with the guides and the crew at our hotel in Paro. It also happens to be Nelle's birthday. There are gifts for her, and for our guides and officials. I appreciate the warm spirits, but I'm getting worried about my finger, particularly its swelling and discoloration.

After an unrestful sleep, I wake with the vestiges of a dream flickering in my brain. In it, an elephant was stepping on my hand, and it hurt like hell. Once I'm conscious, I find no elephant in the room. However, the pain is achingly present. My wedding band is the problem (I'll be careful who I say that to). It's constricting the blood flow to the jammed-up digit, and there is no way to remove it. I assure myself the swelling will eventually subside and the ring will slide off. I get up and pack. By midmorning we have all the gear loaded, and are on the way to our next production location in India.

During the first leg of the flight, the cabin pressure does me no favors. My finger is screaming; I am quietly doing Lamaze breathing. I look out the plane's window, pressing my forehead against the glass, and fantasize about parachuting onto a random Himalayan peak and plunging my hand into the snow. The fingers of my other hand carry their own message: It's time to take my Parkinson's meds. I haven't had this strong or sudden a cue since my arrival in Bhutan.

"How can I miss you if you won't stay away?" I mutter.

We stop in Kathmandu, take on more passengers, and quickly depart for Delhi. A well-dressed Nepali gentleman sits down in the aisle seat next to me. He gives me a polite nod. Then with a furrow in his brow, he glances down at my hand. He meets my eyes and says, "Forgive me, I can't help but notice your finger."

"Yeah," I say. "I banged it up in a fall."

"How long ago was that?" he asks.

"Yesterday afternoon. Tiger's Nest."

"I'm a doctor," he informs me. "May I examine your hand?"

I didn't have any better offers. "Sure," I say. He takes my hand and gently pokes around the ring finger. I wince.

"If you don't remove that ring soon, your finger will be coming off with it." I let out a nervous chuckle. *He's kidding, right?* But his reaction is sober. "When you get to Delhi, you must go directly to the hospital. I'll have the pilot call ahead."

<hr>

We land in Delhi. The doctor confers with Nelle, Nina, and Rudy about which hospital to go to, how to get there, and what to expect upon arrival. He also warns us that traffic will be difficult, even more of an existential nightmare than usual. Today, he reminds us, is the Holi festival, the Hindu holiday that celebrates spring.

We are permitted to jump the line and rush through customs. The production crew stays behind to collect our luggage, while we head to the hospital. We step outside the airport arrivals door, in hopes of spotting our car and driver. I am stopped in my tracks by my introduction to Delhi. Everyone is honking and screaming: the deafening buzz and chatter of what seems, through the haze, to be a million people. Unlike the clear Himalayan ether, the air is so thick with pollution that we choke on it. It feels as if we are actually breathing in solids, and our exhales are reduced to sputters. The lack of visibility is shocking.

The driver holds a "Fox" sign in the middle of traffic. We motion for him to stay there as we make our way to him. The car is splattered with pastel colors, and the driver is a human rainbow. This is what the doctor was referring to when he warned us that this is no ordinary day in Delhi (and we were already prepared to accept that there are no ordinary days in Delhi). On this, the second day of the festival, Rangwali Holi, the custom is to grab fists full of sticky, vividly colored, pastel paint powder and throw it at the face, body, and clothing of any person within range. As we drive to the hospital, clouds of colored powder explode on the windshield: blue for Krishna, the god of love; green for rebirth and new beginnings; red for marriage and fertility; and apparently, for when the going gets fancy, yellow, the color of turmeric. It is a free-for-all. No one is spared. Every caste, gender, and age participates, often with paint loaded into squirt guns and water balloons. Everyone has a piece of the madness.

The Delhi I see out my paint-splattered window is more than I can process, and in no way sufficient to create an understanding. En route to Bhutan last week, we didn't leave the airport on our layover in Delhi; in fact, we didn't leave the lounge. So this is my first experience in India. When I look at the roiling sea of humans, cows, and vehicles, I think back to Thimphu and the ornately costumed citizens waiting patiently for the man in the kiosk to wave them across the street. Clearly, we are in a different country.

As intrigued as I am, the pain in my finger hasn't subsided. With the car windows tightly sealed to keep us from the chaos, we remain our original hues, but we are perspiring in the 100-degree heat. Even with all that sweat, the ring still won't slide off. I wonder about the hospital, but I'm comforted by something my medical friend told me on the plane: "You'll be in good hands. There are more doctors per capita in Delhi than in the United States."

At last, we arrive at the hospital. While Nelle pays the driver, I fumble in my pockets for a bottle of pills. This is the worst time for a shaky hand. Symptoms are starting to show, but I want to be steady for whatever awaits me inside.

India Blue

The emergency intake and adjacent reception area is crowded, but considering the color wars raging outside the doors, it is more orderly than

I expect. An intern leads me to a corridor outside of a presently occupied exam room. Just a few short steps away, a blue man is being treated for
what appears to be trouble breathing. He isn't blue from what ails him, but
from the paint splattered over his skin and clothing. The man's concerned
family, all speaking to him at once, gather around him, striking figures in
green, red, and yellow. *What is it, asthma?* I wonder. *Or a heart attack?*
Comparison and equivalency; who's got it worse? If it is asthma, that's
probably an even trade for an amputated finger. Would my blue friend make
that trade? Not if he knew that the missing finger came with twenty
years of progressive Parkinson's. From my side of the bargain, if it's a heart
attack, no thanks. I think of the maxim "If we were all to put our worst
problem inside of a circle and then allowed to draw one out, we'd all take
our own problem back." I hope he isn't having a heart attack, and I hope
like hell I'm not about to get my finger chopped off.

We enter the next available examining room, with the same setup as
any Western hospital. The doctor takes a preliminary look at my hand.
It's not good. Things have clearly progressed to a tricky place. My finger
is now so swollen and discolored that at first glance it is difficult to see the
ring. It's almost wholly enveloped in engorged tissue. How do you cut it
off without cutting off part of my finger? It just now hits me how much I
love to play guitar.

The doctor asks me a few basic questions about what happened.
He quietly pronounces, "We must get that ring off, or you'll lose your
finger."

"Yeah, I've heard that."

Additional hospital staff members gradually appear. Each seems invested
in coming up with a solution.

It's becoming a hot topic in the E.R., a conundrum that's gone viral
throughout the hospital. What ensues amounts to a Keystone Cops car-
ousel of various staff, from medical doctors to maintenance workers,

each with a different method, some exotic, all ineffective. Hacksaws, wire cutters, tin snips, a disturbing mini-guillotine-like device, petroleum jelly, ghee butter, and other lubricants are all employed, to no avail. I wish I had something to contribute, but I'm stumped. Well, not yet.

An instrument of the file variety finally does the trick. A doctor enters holding a small coil of wire. Her proposal is to feed the wire between my finger and the ring, pull it through until the ends are equidistant, then grab each end and work it like dental floss.

"Whoa," I say. "You're going to floss my finger off."

She explains that the theory is to exert pressure upward and into the metal, until a small groove is established that will allow for a slightly larger and raspier wire to be applied. She goes to work, and ultimately enough room is created for a suitable cutting tool to finish the job. After all of the aborted attempts to set me free, this works. Once the band is removed, there's an instant flush of relief. I'm assured there's no broken bones, only torn ligaments. The ring is a write-off, but I carefully collect the bits and pieces, put them in my pocket, and make plans to have it resoldered in the not-too-distant future.

After we thank everyone, the doctors ask me if I will take photos with them. I'm happy to show off my elaborately bandaged left hand, with its splinted digit. We step outside into the heat and glaring sun of the parking lot. For the second time, I download India. I'm glad we have a few days to spend in Delhi.

Before the group breaks up, I have to ask the intern, "By the way, what happened to the blue guy?"

He is confused. "Blue guy?"

I say, "Yeah, came in about the same time as me? Blue paint? I think he had asthma, maybe allergies."

"Oh, yes," he answers. "That man had a heart attack."

"Is he okay?"

He shakes his head. "He died."

I think of his family washing off the paint. There will be rituals and consolations, much the same as at home, and as different from home as India itself. No comparison.

A week of Zen—gone sideways.

5

DOUBLE BOGEY

Why me? Why did this happen? I have a wife and children, a life that I love. So why was I afflicted with golf?

To take up golf in my forties was ambitious; to do so with Parkinson's disease was delusional. And yet, that's what I did. What buoyed my spirits and stoked my enthusiasm, originally, was this simple concept: By my mid-forties, my physical decline, though not precipitous, was inarguable. I could still do some things well, but not as well as I once did. Golf became the exception. Every time I hit the links, I performed slightly better than I did the last time. Never mind that it could be graded in varying degrees of lousy.

The person most responsible for my entrée into the golfing world was Ed Levy, a fellow Parkinson's patient and an éminence grise on The Michael J. Fox Foundation board. In the early years of our organization, Ed and a few of his Wall Street friends proposed an annual golf tournament to complement the variety of ways we raise funds for research. I was dubious. Wasn't much of a golf fan. Didn't play the game. Always figured there was plenty of time for golf when I'm dead. "Do we really want to do golf events?" I asked. The answer was yes. The outing was a huge success.

I couldn't attend the first year, but as the second year approached, Ed asked if I'd caddy for him. He was older than me, and further along in the progression of his disease. I was much more able-bodied than I am now, so I agreed to do it with a caveat: Instead of lugging Ed's clubs around, I threw them in the back of a cart and volunteered to drive. I had a blast, and the next year, I decided to play.

Ed was the first of many golf mentors, a disparate band of duffers who have dragged me onto the green glare of courses all around the world, from the municipal to the magnificent. There is my neighbor, Teddy, who lives five houses down from me on Long Island, and other seasoned players, like George Stephanopoulos, Harlan Coben, Jimmy Fallon, and Bill Murray. They aren't like dads, whom you don't want to disappoint, but like favorite uncles—the kind who let stuff slide, and who'd sneak you a beer when you were seventeen. The uncles look past my difficulties in playing golf with Parkinson's, and embrace the truth that golf is hell for everyone. We all feel the burn. The joy is not in overcoming or defeating it; instead, it's in surviving it, and settling bets at the nineteenth hole.

Like every gladiator out there on the killing fields, the uncles really only give a shit about their game, not yours or mine. Just keep it moving, and everything's copacetic. Better players don't mind lousy, but they can't abide slow. They're obsessed with completing a round under the time allotted by the course starter. In my case, when the uncs are putting, and I'm still in the fairway bunker, four or five shots off the green, I just pick up the ball, put it in my pocket, and make my way to the next tee. I'm not keeping score, anyway. The uncles approve.

From the start, anyone paying attention could see that I had no affinity for the game. After our first round of nine holes together, my good friend Cam Neely, a founding member of the golf uncles, and an NHL Hall of

Famer (hockey players are famous for being prodigious golfers), summed up my game thusly: "Your problem, Mike"—he paused—"is loft."

"How can I have a problem with loft?" I asked. "I can barely get the ball off the ground."

"No," he said. "L-O-F-T. Lack Of Fucking Talent."

When you're as preternaturally bad as I am, friends, strangers, and concerned groundskeepers are quick to offer annoyingly helpful suggestions. My all-time favorite: "Be still over the ball." *Be still over the ball?* I'd like to be still over my soup! Arnold Palmer once wrote (yes, it's that bad, I'm actually *reading* about golf), "Think of your feet and head as the three apexes of an immovable triangle." Thanks, Arnie. I'll be sure to pack a protractor and a slide rule in my bag, along with my bug spray and nose zinc. And thanks, also, for the refreshing beverage.

Tee-box trigonometry aside, Arnie was probably the ultimate golf uncle for a lot of neophytes. Less approachable, Tiger Woods is not known for sharing his golf wisdom, but he does always promise that on Sunday at the Masters, he will bring his A-game. I could only threaten to bring *a* game.

Tracy was both amused and bemused by all of this. While delighted that I had a new pastime, one that gave me so much pleasure and got me out of the house and moving my body, she had a particular reaction when I would talk about the cheerful bonhomie of the golf uncles, and how they welcomed me into their fold. "Mike, listen. They're crack dealers, only the crack is golf. They got you hooked and reeled you in. I'm happy that you love playing, honey, and I'm happy you made so many friends. But I'm just saying . . . crack."

Breakfast Ball

It's just after sunrise. My friend Teddy from down the block is coming to pick me up in his noisy 1970 Buick Skylark. Where are my silly half-socks?

Where are my good shorts, not the ones from three summers ago that are too small now? I'm on tiptoes in the semi-darkness, trying not to wake Tracy. My wife deserves a peaceful Sunday morning sleep-in, so I try to get my stuff ready the night before. But I always forget something. If I'm making too much noise, it's just because there's a fire in my belly. I'm going golfing.

I check the list: pills, sunscreen, sunglasses, extra tees, shirt, shorts, belt, shoes, and a pair of ankle-cut sports socks. When I sit down to put these on my feet, I notice with chagrin that Nike has decided to label the socks "Left" and "Right." The problem is, I'm holding two lefts. I am perturbed. This feels like a jinx; two left socks. *What do I have, two left feet?* I hear the voice of my dad. "Then there must be a pair of rights somewhere in your sock drawer, son." Switching them out means reentering the bedroom and definitely waking Tracy this time. Just because I'm up at 6:15, doesn't mean she has to be. Or so she said. To hell with it; I'll go with the two left socks. I'm not happy about it, but there it is.

Our tee time is 7:30. Soon, I'm sitting on my porch with my clubs, waiting for Teddy to roll up in his convertible. He does, and a half an hour later, we're on the first tee with the other two in our foursome. It's my favorite time of day: The dew still beads the grass, and the songbirds are in full throat. I pull my lucky driver out of the bag and lead us off. This is the last time I'll go first all day. It's called "the honor system"—the winner of the previous hole has the honor of teeing off at the next. I'm never that guy.

My pills haven't quite kicked in yet, so it takes fifteen attempts to place and balance my ball on the tee. The boys are used to this. I don't ask for their help, and none is offered. I set the ball up, it wobbles, and it rolls off. I repeat; the same result, over and over. I make a joke about occupational therapy. By the time I finally secure the ball in place, I indulge in a silent affirmation. *This is your moment. You know what to do.*

I run through my list of swing thoughts:

NO TIME LIKE THE FUTURE   59

Keep your feet planted on the ground.

Left toe pointed slightly forward.

Soften your knees.

Find your center of gravity.

Chin up.

Pause at the top of the backswing.

Keep your eyes down on the follow-through.

Two left socks . . .

Holy shit! The ball slices right, into the parking lot. "Fore!" Thankfully, I hear no screaming or breaking glass—although I find out later that I almost nailed Dr. Phillips, a big muckety-muck at the club, whom I had only recently convinced to accept me for membership.

I reach into my pocket to pull out a "breakfast ball," the do-over mulligan traditional for first-hole misfires. This time I purge socks from my mind; I forget about my swing. I just think about the moment the club strikes the ball, like a hockey stick and puck. It's all about contact. Don't overthink. I reach back, pause in my backswing, and deliver the clubhead with sufficient force to send the ball soaring 180 yards, straight down the fairway, a mere pitching wedge away from the green. I turn to my friends. "I know, I know. Any asshole can hit the second shot."

Every time I play can either be the best round or the worst. Today, it has been both. The clock at the eighteenth hole tells us we're ten minutes ahead of schedule. Everyone is satisfied and can hold their heads up in the clubhouse, but not me. I'm thinking: *Well, that's it. My last round of golf. Why am I wasting everyone's time?* But there was that breakfast ball, the one that set me up for a possible birdie (I went on to four-putt). Still, one to grow on.

Golf celebrates your vulnerabilities, and shames you for having the temerity to even pick up a club. Yet, should I get a phone call, text, or email that three buddies are looking for a fourth, I'll drop everything. One well-played hole in a round of eighteen—if successfully negotiated for birdie, par, or even an honest bogey—can lure me back for another round of abuse; all memory of seventeen disastrous holes magically erased.

Mark Twain famously described the game of golf as "a good walk spoiled." For me, it's more of a good shuffle-tumble-lurch. With balance issues, I am prone to falls, one of the few people who can injure himself while putting. Golf summons up the same resolve that I rely upon in managing my Parkinson's. I could easily create a Venn diagram exploring the nexus between golf and life with PD: They overlap in hubris and humility, delusion and desire, futility and resilience. I just deal with whatever presents itself. Sometimes I end up in the bunker, in the deep rough, or in the water. Carry on. If you're going to do something, just do it. And don't use too much club.

A commonly asked question on the links is: "What's your handicap?" My answer: "Isn't it obvious?" The sport and disability have met and intermingled in my experiences as a golfer/patient, and an impatient golfer.

Who knew that Ed Levy's invitation to caddy would introduce me to the unexpected joy of the world's most frustrating sport? I'm grateful . . . I think. A decade later, PD will force Ed to hang up his clubs. Through the years that I continue playing, the game becomes an escape, a relief and release from preoccupation with my health situation. When you're golfing, all you can think about is golf.

Not long after Ed's retirement from the game, my own health will relegate my clubs to storage, for a while or perhaps forever. In a way, Parkinson's pitted itself against golf. For a time there, golf was winning; my game was getting better at a faster pace than my Parkinson's was getting worse. Not exactly advanced analytics. But eventually, the data will turn against me.

6

LOCO MOTION

I used to defy gravity on a daily basis, and I could run like a quarter horse. Now I'm fifty-eight years old, and I perambulate like I'm ninety. No, wait—I know a couple of ninety-year-olds who jog, for Christ's sake. They leave me standing in the dust, while their jet stream tips me over. An old guy with a cane hustled past my office the other day. Admiring the rhythm of his stick work, my only thought was, *Look at that son-of-a-bitch go!* This is what I aspire to now: I want to move like that guy.

But really, I want to move like I did as a kid.

Slippery Quick

In 1971, when I was ten, my dad retired from the Canadian Armed Forces. We left Ontario, his last posting, to return to British Columbia where my family had roots. We moved from army housing into an apartment complex, across the street from a strip mall and a liquor store. Within weeks,

I had explored every back alley, side street, and shortcut in and around the neighborhood. Having memorized the route from our complex to the apartment where my aunt and uncle lived, five miles away, I thought nothing of making the trek by myself, unannounced and unaccompanied. Once I arrived, I would enjoy a cold glass of tap water while Aunt Marilyn called my mom to report my location.

Back then, I'd just start walking. Walk to school, walk through the woods, walk to the movies. I rode my bike, too, and I could skate. A typical Canadian kid, I played hockey from the age of six. I was built for speed, low to the ground, spontaneous and impulsive. Nimble, with panther reflexes. In hockey, or in sports in general, they describe someone with quick legs as having "great wheels." The legendary Montreal Canadien, Guy Lafleur, had wheels. *I* had wheels.

Lafleur also had "hands"; that is, he had a facility to stickhandle, to move the puck on the blade of the stick in strange and magical ways. That allowed him to become a proficient scorer. I didn't have hands, nor did I have what coaches call "hockey sense," in that I couldn't see the game in a visionary way—unlike Wayne Gretzky, who could deliver a puck not to where a teammate was, but to where they were going to be. I didn't have much of a shot, either, but man, could I fly. I patrolled the ice with such speed, agility, and flair that you could be easily fooled into thinking I was actually doing something. I loved the movement, being a blur.

A perpetual motion machine, I was constantly running, jumping, hurtling, sprinting, skipping a rope in the boxing gym. Scrambling over rocks at the shoreline, casting and reeling, pitching and hitting, skiing and body surfing. Climbing up the brick wall to the roof of the liquor store to retrieve an errant street-hockey ball. Sneaking my arm over a date's shoulder at the movies.

George Bernard Shaw said that youth is wasted on the young, but it wasn't wasted on me. I just didn't know that I'd go straight from young to old.

Moving Pieces

From childhood into adulthood, I continued to exploit my physicality, not only for fun, but for profit. Over the course of my career, I've executed pratfalls, shoulder rolls, and fake fights—occasionally landing a wayward punch and taking one in return. I've leapt off of buildings, flown on wires, and skateboarded through studio back lots. I've been choreographed by the Broadway director Herb Ross, who turned a stroll through an office building in *The Secret of My Success* into a scene out of a Harold Lloyd movie. Herb challenged me to navigate a maze of file cabinets with extended drawers, stuttering elevator doors, the mops and buckets of maintenance workers, and other workplace hazards (all of this, regrettably, to the tune of "Walking on Sunshine").

As a director, Brian De Palma could not be more different from Herb Ross, but Brian created his own form of choreography. He's famous for his extended Steadicam shots; minutes-long, continuous takes. For example, the camera might follow an actor along a hallway, down a staircase, out the door, to the street, and onto a moving bus—all in one shot. I did one of these De Palma specials in Thailand, while filming *Casualties of War*. It was, in its own way, some of the most physically demanding work I'd ever done, and it involved nothing more arduous than walking. My character, a raw recruit, engages in nervous chatter with a fellow soldier; an existential conversation about how easy it is to get your ass killed in Vietnam. We do this as we trudge along a rutted dirt road, all hell breaking loose in the background. A village burns steadily, the flames fed by occasional explosions. Helicopters zip in and out, landing and taking off. Army personnel pass through the frame, firing weapons and hauling dead and wounded onto the choppers. All the while, pages and pages of dialogue have to be delivered with exquisite precision. Amid the manufactured bedlam, a too-quick footstep or a misspoken line means an entire scene is blown, and ten minutes of footage is lost. And that would be on you. "Back to one."

With all of the horrific sounds—the gunshots, the bombs, the close whirr of helicopters—the most terrifying one was Brian yelling, "Cut!" before the scene was meant to end.

Back on safer ground, as Alex Keaton, I learned how to maneuver through a scene and around a set in the moment. I would fly through doors and slide across countertops with my hands in my pockets, somehow willing myself to float from camera mark to camera mark. I'd glide and spin on a rolling office chair across the proscenium of the kitchen set. It was basically all a dance, although I'm no dancer.

One of the early scenes in the pilot episode of *Spin City* takes place in a small Manhattan apartment bedroom. My character, Deputy Mayor Mike Flaherty, and his girlfriend, Ashley, a political reporter, are in a back-and-forth dialogue about moving in together permanently. A few double entendres, a few sexy eye-flutters, and the scene turns romantic. For what Mike has in mind next, he needs to get from one side of the room, over the bed, to the other, and have his sweatpants off by the time he lands. I propose to the director, Tommy Schlamme (a legendary TV director with one of the best monikers in show business), that I do this by flipping over the bed, with Ashley lying in it, and removing my sweatpants in midair.

"Okay," he said. "I'll buy it. But how the hell do you know you can do that?"

"I don't. But I think I can. Let me try."

"Do I get a vote?" Carla Gugino, who played Ashley, spoke up. "Just don't land on me."

"And don't break your neck," Tommy said. "I'd have to fill out a lot of forms."

Somehow, I managed to execute the maneuver flawlessly, to the delight and relief of everyone involved. It was a flying start to our pilot episode.

PD Paradox

To me, movement always represented freedom. It was a couple of years into my Parkinson's diagnosis that I recognized "movement disorder" as an accepted handle for my affliction. I'm sure it had been used in materials I'd read, or mentioned by doctors I consulted, but in time, the full meaning of those words sank in. Mine is not a mental disorder or an emotional one, although these issues can develop. It is neurological, and manifests in a corruption of movement. Some people will focus on the slight palsy, the tremoring of fingers and limbs. That's certainly a part of it. But at least in my experience, these symptoms have become more manageable over time. Much more difficult to acknowledge and accept is the *diminishment* of movement. Absent a chemical intervention, Parkinson's will render me frozen, immobile, stone-faced, and mute—entirely at the mercy of my environment. For someone for whom motion equals emotion, vibrancy, and relevance, it's a lesson in humility.

On the upside, I have found that I can play mind games with myself. I employ a strategy I've used throughout my life—if I don't know I can do something physically, I just pretend that I can. Fake it until I make it. Eight times out of ten, it works. The remaining 20 percent? Stitches, broken bones, humiliation.

The Impatient Patient

Someone who helps me demark the lines and boundaries I face in life is Dr. Susan Bressman. She's my neuro and movement disorder specialist; also a brilliant researcher, an internationally recognized expert in Parkinson's disease, and a valued advisor to our Foundation. We're lucky to have her on our team, and I'm grateful for her personal attention. She's always thorough in my one-hour check-ups, during which she assesses my present disposition and rate of progression, audits my reported reactions to medications, and monitors my cognitive skills and mental acuity. It can be exhausting. Sometimes I'm "on" during the examinations, and sometimes I'm "off," all of which is duly observed and noted. I wish that everyone could have such careful consideration of their illness as I do with Sue.

As I leave her office after each appointment, I know she's standing in the hallway behind me, assessing the quality of my stride. When I think about walking, a word that now comes to mind is "deliberate." I have to plan every step I take; no extraneous side trips or wasted effort. I have to think about the way I sit in a chair: Am I settled in the right way? I do an inventory of where my limbs are. All of this calculation and deliberation is rigorous work. Physical tasks are made more difficult by the need to break them down into all of their components. The required mental work is harder than the physical effort. I need to think about every step, which demands intense focus.

I have to show up—although it would be so easy *not* to. Some days, I'm done with it all. I don't want to count my steps. I don't want to acknowledge what's worse today, or what will inevitably get worse down the road. It's exhausting to parse out what is Parkinson's, and what is attributable to other factors.

Some things I can't do because I'm fifty-eight. Is that old age? It was when I was twenty-one, which feels like five minutes ago.

Down on the Corner

Unlike when I was twenty-one and living in a roach-infested studio apartment in L.A., I now reside in a prewar building on the Upper East Side of Manhattan. Efforts have been made to modernize the property, or at least acquire modern accessories. For example, an abandoned, oversized, basement laundry room, replete with vestigial washers and dryers from the 1950s, has been cleaned out, renovated, and is now a residents' gym. This is where I receive physical therapy.

My PT, Ryan Orser, while physically imposing, is wholly personable, funny and engaging. An accomplished college lacrosse player and a big fan of his hometown Buffalo Bills, he brings an athlete's perspective to his work. He knows his stuff—the name of every bone, muscle, ligament, and tendon, and how they all work together (or don't). I ask Ryan how he would describe the work he does with Parkinson's patients. "I mean, it's not purely *physical* therapy, right? There's something else going on," I say.

He cracks an impish grin (if the word "impish" can be applied to someone that huge). "It's *like* physical therapy—if the therapist had a mother who is a psychologist, a father who is an ergonomist, a brother who is a dancer, and a mind that is perpetually fifteen."

"Works for me."

My office is around the corner from our apartment, so to get from the office to the home gym, I have to go outside, hang a right, go about thirty feet, take another right for forty feet, and enter the lobby doors under the canopy. This used to be a piece of real estate I could cover without a second's thought, nothing more than a short commute, or the last steps of the trip home from the coffee shop on Madison Avenue, or the bookshop on the corner. It's now the Bermuda Triangle, or more accurately, the Devil's Right Angle.

That's where Ryan comes in. Before each workout, he meets me at the office and we discuss what we're going to do that day, therapy-wise. First priority: laying out a strategy for negotiating the 350 steps from my exterior office door, into my apartment building, and down the stairs to the gym, factoring in variables like the weather, my current "on-off" status, and the time of day. Sounds simple, and some days it is; but on other days, like today, it's a perilous odyssey worthy of Ulysses.

Just stepping out the door is tricky. To make an immediate right necessitates a quick glance to the left to check for oncoming pedestrian traffic. The first step is crucial; I want to make sure it's not complicated by passers-by. There is no such thing in my world as a "quick glance" anymore; it requires my whole body, including my feet, to shift. Seeing that all is clear, I turn right, into the wind. Our particular corner, whether it's airflow vectors or just the shape of our building juxtaposed against the building across the street, confronted by the stone walls of Central Park, conspires to create the most blustery city corner this side of Chicago. Gusts of up to fifty miles per hour have literally knocked me down in recent winters. Even without the blowback, it's freezing today in New York. Sidewalks are slick and icy, and frost heaves have warped the pavement, creating dangerous lips and ledges. The corner always seems to be jammed up with life forms, whether a pet owner dragging his cardigan-sweatered French bulldog out for a pee, or on nicer days, a young teacher shepherding twelve tethered preschoolers.

The second right turn can be a deal-breaker. I've fallen here many times, leaving a patina of knee skin on the concrete. Having found my way around it, I'm now faced with an even more precipitous downhill jaunt into the lobby. The pace is quicker today, so my stride is shorter. The frost has done its damage here, too, so there are countless toe-catchers waiting to drop me if I shuffle. My reflex is to close down my hips, in the hope that it will control my pace. The actual result is a limiting of my options. Another risk is that I'll run into a gaggle of my neighbors, waiting for taxis or unloading groceries from their cars (or at least supervising doormen as they schlep bags inside). The temptation is to stop and say hi, be friendly. *Wrong. Do not stop. Do not make eye contact. Do not engage. It's clear you're struggling; you've got a cane, for Christ's sake. They'll understand.* I step up, in and away, and take a left this time, to the service stairway that leads down to the basement.

The running of that gauntlet, believe it or not, is followed by an hour of physical therapy.

Brain Sweat

Core work, crunches, sit-ups, bicycle kicks, the dreaded ab chair—we always start off with the fun stuff. "Okay, walk over here. Hips forward, shoulders back, don't drag that left foot," Ryan commands. But while I'm concentrating on lifting my left foot, I hyperextend my right knee.

Damn.

"It's okay, we're going to work on that later," Ryan says. A willing student, I work my ass off, but I get a little cranky and whiny as I'm put through my paces.

Ryan flops a rubber mat down on the faux pine floor and says, "Toe-touches. Right knee up, left leg down, touch your right foot with your left hand, then switch. Give me twenty of those."

It takes me a second to picture the movement, even though I've done this a hundred times before. But I want to be sure, because I know what's coming next. I do one. I do two. I do three. And here it comes: Ryan says, "Who's the sixteenth president of the United States?"

I grunt, reaching out to grab my left toe. "Lincoln? I don't know—I'm Canadian."

"Correct. What's (3 x 3) minus (7 + 2)?" He's jumping all over my brain, in the areas where I store information. I hesitate and grab my left toe twice.

"Zero," I grunt. "Nada. Zilch." While all of this is going on, he's laying out a course of pylons, two paces apart. They zigzag the length of the gym floor. I stand in front of the first one, get my balance, take a big step, and slalom my way through the course. I have to go slowly and carefully. On my second step, he starts in again.

"Name the planets in order from the sun."

I get the Mercury/Venus/Earth/Mars intro out of the way, but what's next—Jupiter or Saturn?

"Jupiter?" I take a guess.

"Right," Ryan says. "Don't hyperextend. Loosen that knee up. Strike your heel. Slow your pace. Concentrate."

"I can't concentrate," I complain. "You're sabotaging me." Then I blurt out: "Saturn, Uranus, Neptune." I turn, my left foot dragging into a pylon, knocking it over and nearly bringing myself down with it. "And sometimes Pluto."

Ryan laughs and says, "I bet you're thinking: 'You ask me to do all of these goddamn things. I can't even stand in front of the toilet and pee straight.'"

"At least I still stand," I answer.

After another forty-five minutes of working out—treadmill, rowing machine, and a selection of stretching exercises approved by Torquemada—today's session is done. We collect our things, put on coats and hats, and prepare to retrace the series of rights and lefts (mostly lefts this time) back to the office. Even exiting through the gym's door is an opportunity to reinforce my therapy. These kinds of transitions cause my brain to hiccup; passing through doorways poses a challenge, depending on what I'm stepping out of and into. I do a quick reset, and then proceed on steady legs. We opt to take the staircase to the lobby instead of waiting for the service elevator. It may seem counterintuitive, but stairs are easier for me to negotiate than flat surfaces. My problem is not strength, it's coordination. Stair treads are plain in their visual language. They prescribe the height to which I have to raise my foot, as well as how far forward and how flat my footfall should be. The handrail doesn't hurt, either.

Ryan keeps talking. "Do you remember how you were sitting when I first met you?"

"I don't know—on my ass?"

"Yeah, but you also had your leg on the ottoman. The other leg was on the ground, pushed into the corner of the couch. You had one outstretched arm here, and the other arm there. Just to balance, you had to touch all of those points of contact."

"Like Ralph Macchio doing the crane in *Karate Kid*."

Ryan nods. "You were like that because you wanted to pay attention to our conversation. The rest of us don't have to worry about what our bodies are doing when we talk to people, but you really need to focus. Movement can be intensely distracting."

We reach the heavy brass-and-glass lobby door. He holds it open and I pass through without hesitation. "Okay," Ryan says from behind me. "Let's take this next part slowly. Stop. Set your feet. Think about where you're going: a short uphill to the corner; turn; pause again. Count your steps."

The bright sun bounces off concrete, the afternoon traffic tumbles downtown, and the sidewalks are lightly populated. I nod, take a medium yoga breath, and I'm on my way.

"One . . . two . . . three. . . ." Ryan is counting aloud beside me, but out of my line of sight. "Six . . . seven. . . ."

Suddenly, I get distracted. *Does that lady have a dog in her handbag?* My left leg hyperextends, and I start to pitch toward the building's sidewalk garden. In a second, Ryan's arm shoots out to grab and steady me. He catches me under the armpit and pulls me upright again. Giving me a grim smile, he nudges me forward. "Eight . . . nine . . . ten . . ." He counts a little louder.

What Ryan's doing is simple. He's trying to teach my mind to perform one exercise while my body performs another. I need to create new pathways in my brain, new ways of compartmentalizing actions and words. Basically, what he's teaching me is not only how to walk and talk at the same time, but how to safely think about other things while still being aware of the kinetics involved in moving from place to place.

I find myself reciting tongue-twisters—*Fuzzy wuzzy wasn't fuzzy, was he?*—when I do pushups and bicycle crunches in my office. If she sells seashells, then I'm buying, because this stuff is working. I may one day master multitasking. But I'd prefer Ryan go easy on the math.

7

UNSAFE AT ANY SPEED

I love my mother too much to give her a hug.

I have traveled the width of the country and across an international border to surprise Mom. It's Canadian Thanksgiving, and more importantly, her ninetieth birthday. Unleashing an emotional surprise on a ninety-year-old is a dodgy proposition at best, but I have pulled this kind of unannounced pop-up with her before.

Ten years ago, my brother, Steve, and I delivered room service to her hotel suite in Belfast, Northern Ireland, where she was touring with my sisters, Jackie and Kelli. The day they left on their trip, Steve and I were talking on the phone, and one of us came up with the outlandish idea to fly to Belfast the following day and surprise them. It was so last-minute and tightly scheduled, the only flights we could get required Steve to fly from Vancouver to JFK, and then immediately transfer by car to Newark, New Jersey, for our overseas flight.

There's no easy way to get from airport to airport without taking a diagonal trip across Manhattan. I picked up Steve via a car service, and soon we were trapped in metro New York traffic, crawling through the Lincoln Tunnel and then on to the terminal in Newark, with only a few minutes to spare. An off-duty airport cop volunteered to expedite us through security, and blazed the shortest trail to the gate, luggage in tow. He put his foot in the cabin door as the flight attendant was closing it, and tossed the two of us onto the plane. We made it to Belfast just in time for breakfast.

There was a higher purpose to our madness—we had always planned to take a trip abroad as a family, but my father was no longer with us, and our older sister, Karen, had passed away a couple of years earlier. My two surviving sisters, Kelli, and Jackie, had organized this pilgrimage with Mom to her ancestral homeland in Northern Ireland. Steve and I saw this as an opportunity to affirm family ties. We wanted in on Phyllis Piper Fox's return to a home she'd never been to before. Mom's reaction, upon realizing that the gents bearing her room service tray were her two sons, was a mixture of shock and delight.

Now, ten years later, my big brother and I hatch another plan. Steve and his family live only a few miles from Mom, and he often drops by to do handiwork and chores around her high-rise condo. He tells her that he'll be over the next morning, and that he'll call from the lobby, so she can buzz him up. When she opens the door, surprise! It won't be Steve, it will be me. This works to perfection, except Mom doesn't answer the door, my sister Kelli does. It's probably better this way—we avoid the shock of a nose-to-nose reveal, which might give my mother a heart attack. Kelli steps back. Mom, rising from the sofa in the living room, sees me, and brings her hands to her face. She lets out a sort of squeak. "Hey, Mom. Hope you weren't expecting room service."

In the excitement of the reunion, I fear stumbling, careening, and slamming into my ninety-year-old mother, taking us both out. Eight to ten steps from the threshold of the door to the sofa, I agonize over each footfall. Wherever I land, I need to be stable before I go in for a hug—careful not to lean too far forward, which would push her back; but instead, managing to receive her in a way that allows room for me to adjust. *For Chrissake, just don't knock her down.* At the very least, I could re-break her hip.

After a long and slightly trembling hug, I step back, as if to take her in, but mostly to keep her safe by keeping my distance. She looks fit and happy. Me, I'm just happy.

Over thirty years of Parkinson's, I've progressed into something dangerous. I've been weaponized. Most recently, my mobility and balance issues have definitely worsened. I struggle with consistency, establishing and maintaining a steady rhythm in my gait; thus, the careful attention paid to the quick trip from the door to my mother. Paradoxically, standing for any length of time is also a wobbly proposition.

And it's not just Mom whom I endanger, merely by the slightest intrusion into her personal space. My mother-in-law, Corky, who is a contemporary of my mom, also is at risk from me, and needs a careful approach. In fact, New Yorkers, tourists and random citizens, just busying their way down Madison Avenue, blithely tapping on their cell phones, have no idea that a tornado of terror is limping in their direction. I have to be vigilant, careful not just for myself, but for anyone who is unfortunate enough to be in my unpredictable path.

Sometimes I view the world as a pinball game, and I am a steel ball fired from the spring plunger, trying desperately not to light up any buttons on my way to the flipper doors.

Weirdly, I have dreams about this dearth of kinetic self-control. One goes like this: I am rounding the street corner on my way to my apartment building, holding a vial of Parkinson's meds. I stumble and slam into a mailbox, whereupon the capsules spill onto the sidewalk. I stoop to collect the pharmaceuticals, then look up to see a dog walker with a teeming pack of Upper East Side hounds moving in to gobble up the drugs. God knows what kind of damage that would do to a canine's insides—although given the neighborhood, the dogs are probably on some kind of antidepressant already. I wake up with Gus licking my face.

The Uncertainty Principle

The German theoretical physicist Werner Heisenberg established a number of laws and principles that, along with the work of a coterie of other geniuses, led to the creation of quantum mechanics. Heisenberg's work earned him the 1932 Nobel Prize in Physics.

The theory that bears his name is Heisenberg's Uncertainty Principle, which states that *the more precisely the position of a particle is determined, the less precisely its momentum can be known, and vice versa.* Heisenberg describes exactly the conundrum that we Parkinsonians face in dealing with gait. I cannot determine my position and my velocity at the same time. It's an unsolvable problem; people caution me to slow down as I shuffle-step-stumble forward, but they don't realize that it's an impossible request. I simply can't feel how fast I'm going. Moreover, my brain won't let my body stop until it finds a safe position—and it can't find a safe position while I'm still moving. This relates directly to Heisenberg's Principle. Joseph Heller would also lay claim to it as a classic *Catch-22*: it's a dilemma from which there is no escape, because of mutually conflicting conditions.

Here's how I visualize it: If my body was sectioned into tenths, horizontally, each tenth would be traveling at its own speed, and not in any sequence that makes sense. I am never still long enough to gauge my body's position as a whole. Adding to the chaos, the quickening of pace and simultaneous shortening of stride (cardinal features of advanced Parkinson's) sabotage my journey. My pace quickens beyond the brain neurons' capacity to fire, and I can suddenly lose my balance. Nine times of out ten, I manage to panic-dance all my horizontal sections, in the hopes that they'll all fall into line and recover equilibrium before I steamroll somebody.

And people think Parkinson's disease is all about tremor. I thought that once, too.

Surprise, Again

I savor the time in Canada with my mother and my family, especially when there's a reason to celebrate. The day after I arrive, Steve, Jackie, Kelli, and I take Mom to lunch at a local pizza place in Burnaby, the suburb of Vancouver where I grew up. It's a family favorite; we've been going there since we were kids. It's been spruced up since then, with red leather banquettes instead of picnic tables, but the pizza still tastes like sixth grade. We order a few pies and some soft drinks, and then the fun starts. Mom's cell phone rings.

"Helloo?" she answers.

"Hey, Nana. I just wanted to wish you a happy birthday."

Mom points to her phone and tells us, "It's Sam, calling from Los Angeles."

She goes back to her grandson. "Oh, thank you, sweetie! I bet you know about my surprise—your dad's here. Do you want to talk to him?"

"No, just have him call me. Actually, never mind. He can't call me. I have his phone."

With that, Sam walks around the corner to our table.

We all look to Mom. Again, the hands to the face and the tiny squeak; again, thank god, no myocardial infarction. Sam hands me back my cell phone, sits down next to my mother, and wraps her in a hug. Nothing dangerous about it—a safe, stable, normal hug.

After lunch, my ninety-year-old mother drives us to a bowling alley. We bowl two games, and Mom kicks our asses. Yes, my mother still bowls, and she still drives. Every few years, I buy her a Volkswagen Passat, which she operates safely, without incident.

I turned in my car keys almost a decade ago. In my twenties, I owned five kinds of sports cars, and a few variations on the Range Rover. I could match-light a cigarette going 80 mph in my Ferrari, with the top down. With marriage and babies came four-door sedans and child car seats; no more sports cars. And then, on my thirty-fifth birthday, Tracy led me outside our apartment building on Central Park West, where I found my gift curbside: a red 1967 Mustang convertible, with vintage plates that declared it a registered antique. *It was six years younger than me.*

I zipped around in that car for years, until my early fifties, when I found that my right foot was consistently and rhythmically pumping the throttle. The car would accelerate, decelerate; accelerate, decelerate, lurching down the road as I struggled to control it. That will take the sexy right out of a red convertible. Another safety issue: my increasing uneasiness about the proximity of other cars on the roadway, a PD-related spatial perception deficit. I also developed a tendency to steer in whatever direction I was looking. All of this convinced me that—despite the fact that I still had a valid driver's license—I was unsafe at any speed.

My mother, on the other hand, manages just fine. Being born during the Depression and coming of age during World War II made Mom tough, determined, and indefatigable. When my daughter Esmé celebrated her bat mitzvah, my mother insisted on flying to New York, while still recovering from a broken hip. Despite her doctor's firm remonstrations, she wasn't going to miss the celebration. That's my mom. She loves life, and her passions belie her age.

Mom helps me to not think of age as a metric. Who's to say what constitutes the span of a life? When you're one hundred and you pass away, no one says, "What happened?" Your demise is considered overdue. You were living on bonus time, anyway. But there are people like my mother and mother-in-law who are exceptions to this trope. Mom and Corky remain vital and active, and they're not going anywhere soon. Energetic and engaged in their nineties, they are still the architects of their own lives. In my fifties, I'm envious.

8

EXILE ON PAIN STREET

New Year's Eve, 2017

Turks and Caicos, British Overseas Territory

Keith Richards, drink in hand, a massive skull ring tapping the crystal of his cocktail glass, lights a fresh cigarette off the cherry of his last. "Foxy"—his voice is a warm cackle—"Happy New Year."

"Same to you, Keith."

In actual fact, I feel anything but happy at the moment. While our family is vacationing at a celebrity-dense resort in Turks and Caicos during Christmas week, I am ailing from a pinched sciatic nerve, exacerbated by a recent fall in the hallway of my New York office. It is so painful, I can't even walk on the powdery sand without enduring, with each tentative step, a dragon pissing fire down the back of my leg. For the rest of the week, the closest I get to the ocean is the Dune Bar, and I don't drink. I sit like a mope, gazing beachward, sucking on a virgin piña colada, the irony not lost that in spite of my abstemiousness, I still have a fair chance of sliding off my barstool. In that bar, I now wait with Keith Richards, swashbuckling pirate king, immortal rock god, and Rolling freaking Stone, for the New Year's Eve fireworks. I'm not worthy.

The crowd picks up the countdown. At one, there's a sizzling *whoosh* and a loud riot of light in the night sky. Keith tilts his head up, his lined and weathered visage captured in a flash portrait, lit by a burst of white phosphorous. *Oh god, Keith Richards looks better than I feel.*

———

Vacations, particularly family vacations, by definition, remove us from the regular patterns and rhythms of our lives: We're vacating the everyday. We seek enjoyment and relaxation. Ours has always been a family on the move, and we've always loved traveling together. Now with the kids being older—two out of college, one soon to graduate, and one still in high school—it's more important than ever for us to spend downtime with each other, and to catch up on how wings are unfolding outside of the nest.

We travel for a number of special occasions and milestone celebrations, often in the company of other families and friends. Here in the Turks and Caicos, we are with good friends and neighbors, the Schenkers, with their two sons and their daughter, Ally, who is so close to our girls that we call her "the third twin." We also engage in adventure travel, one-off trips to bucket list destinations, with more of a focus on discovery than recovery. Then there are those treasured places we revisit year after year. Familiarity breeds contentment. Holidays—especially Christmas and New Year's—provide an opportunity to gain some perspective on the past year. However stressed or harried or exciting or dull our lives have been up to that point, we relish the comfort of an established retreat. We luxuriate in the sameness, although the sameness is becoming elusive. It's the same family, but my place within it has shifted.

I depend on Tracy more than ever. Every aspect of my life, every action, movement, or emotion, is colored not only by the way I process what's happening with my health challenges, but by the way Tracy processes and reacts to it. I wouldn't be here now, in whatever shape, were it not for Tracy's infinite capacity to accept me as I am in the moment.

FOMO

Unfortunately, at the moment, I'm pissed off and in pain in paradise. And not for the first time, I'm experiencing FOMO. Not a frequent participant in social media, I came late to these Instagram acronyms. The first one I ever used was in response to a Tweet; someone was mocking Parkinson's. I asked Sam how I should reply. "SMH," he instructed. "Trust me." When the original author Tweeted an apology, along with praise for my brilliance, I asked Sam (who was very pleased with himself) what I had said. "Shaking My Head," he told me.

"FOMO" came later. I first heard it used, in relation to me, from Aquinnah. The chatter of my daughters' voices in the hallway of our apartment had me scrambling for my cane and heading out there just in time to see that the impromptu confab was already over. The girls had scattered. Trailing behind, Aquinnah saw me before she turned into her room. "What are you guys talking about?" I blurted out. "I feel like stuff is always getting by me."

"Aw, Dad. You have FOMO," Aquinnah explained.

"I have what? FOMO? Sounds like a fungus." I quickly sniffed my armpits.

"Fear of Missing Out," she clarified.

It's a clever summing-up of a true concern of mine, and on this particular vacation, FOMO is a day-to-day reality. I sit at the bar or poolside, waiting for everyone to show up for lunch or dinner. When they do, I'm like a receptacle—a hamper suddenly filled with used beach towels, none of them mine. I experience the adventures of the family only through their recounting. Not that they abandon me; I do get occasional company pool-side. But I insist they go and enjoy the environs.

Things had been changing over the years, but this trip seems to be tell-ing me that I'm crossing into new territory.

Déja Voodoo

For us, being in this same place at roughly the same time over successive years provides a core sample of life, a layered history of the evolving jour-ney of a family, observed in a specific context: the year Sam sliced his foot badly on a sand-buried conch shell and reacted with a calm stoicism that he wouldn't have been capable of two or three years earlier; seven-year-old Aquinnah and Schuyler, along with Ally, sharing a beach chair and read-ing *Amelia Bedelia*; then seeing the three girls—now twentysomethings—lounging poolside, sipping piña coladas; Esmé, the chameleon, in a new and even more wonderful version of herself. I turn each page of the mem-ory book, beach vacation edition.

Such recollections make me aware of the gradual diminishment of my physical identity. A decade ago, trips to Turks and Caicos would include jet skiing, waterskiing, deep-sea fishing, and tossing a football on the beach with my son and daughters, and the sons and daughters of our friends. Don't get me wrong; there is still a lot to do, and much of the time my favorite thing to do is nothing at all. But I realize that my options have narrowed.

I'm also sensitive to the reactions of hotel staff and regular guests of the resort, with whom I interact year after year. They greet me and say, "How are you?" Regardless of how I respond, I can see them looking me over, doing the math, and deciding for themselves just how well I'm doing. If I detect a sense of sadness or concern, or even alarm, I don't give it much weight. But still, my response—"I'm doing great, really good, thanks"—can be a bit forced.

Things had been unusually difficult for the months leading up to this year's trip: weakness in my limbs, tremendous pain along my sciatic nerve, and a burning sensation on the skin around my abdomen and lower chest, menacing and uncomfortable, like a steel wool sweater. I went to see my dermatologist. There was no rash or other obvious reason for these symptoms, so she sent me to see my neurologist, who diagnosed neurofibromyalgia, a chronic disorder affecting the way my brain processes pain signals. Ironically, countering this nagging pain was a *lack* of feeling, a numbness, in certain areas on my legs and lower back.

Added to this, my recent propensity for falling, in various categories: big, looping, hyperextended, "Ministry-of-Silly-Walks" falls; face-planting due to festination (where I'm tiptoeing and leaning "over my skis"); and plain old tripping due to foot-dragging and irregular gait. The latter two are Parkinson's disease, but the first, the big dramatic tumbles, are linked to something else.

During the holiday in Turks and Caicos, the situation becomes untenable. I need to get back to New York, and figure out what is going on with my health. This means I have to tell Tracy that we must cut the holiday short. If I expect my wife—who loves the beach and the ocean, the sun and the friends and the family, and luckily, me—to hesitate, try to find some compromise, or come up with a plan to stay a couple more days, I am wrong. She immediately says, "No, we should go home. I've been missing you on this vacation." Then she breaks into the Animals' "We Gotta Get Out of This Place." Although I didn't anticipate there would be singing, deep down, I knew she'd be with me. She doesn't hesitate; she holds me for a minute, and with a kiss, is off to tell the kids to start packing.

I love that she clearly gets it. She's responsive, not reactive. It's not that Tracy "feels my pain"; it's that she acknowledges it, and would do anything to relieve it. We try to accept life on life's terms. I've relied on Tracy's acceptance more and more, as my own has begun to waver.

When I was diagnosed with Parkinson's in 1991, Tracy and I were not even thirty years old, and newly married with a young son. I had been experiencing muscle pain and a slight tremor in my finger, and on Tracy's urging, I went to see a neurologist. After a cursory series of dexterity tests, he confidently diagnosed me with young onset Parkinson's disease. I couldn't process what he was saying; only snippets of his pronouncement got through. I do recall him telling me that I might be able to work for ten more years. I was twenty-nine.

I went home to tell Tracy the news. I didn't know how to sneak up on it, so I just laid it out there. "I have Parkinson's." She started to cry, and I started to cry. We held each other in the doorway to our bedroom. When we stepped apart, our faces were painted with similar expressions, something beyond shock. Certainly, that was there, but so was puzzlement. We were sad and scared and confused. We didn't know what to expect, or when to expect it. How fast it would progress. What it would mean to me as a husband and a father, as an actor, and as a person.

Tracy has had the best (or worst) possible view on the disease, and how it has affected me and our family. She has also availed me of her mind, her shoulder, and most important, her heart. She cares about me. That seems banal, and something that should be taken as a given. But I don't only feel that, I know that. And every now and then, without her being aware of it, I've witnessed random acts of her devotion.

There was a flight from the States to Europe. I had the window seat, Tracy had the aisle. It was nighttime, or at least, the airline wanted it to be nighttime, so they had closed the window shades and turned down the lights. It had been a long flight, and I needed to get up and stretch my legs.

Tracy was asleep; I tried not to disturb her as I awkwardly crawled over her reclined chair. When I returned to our row, she was still deeply asleep, so I took an empty seat across the aisle and watched her dream. After some time passed, there was a singular, solitary burst of turbulence. The plane rocked hard, with a metallic growl that resonated.

Tracy sat bolt upright, eyes suddenly wide, and immediately looked to her left to see that my seat was empty. In an instant, she had her blanket off, her seat belt unlatched, and was on her feet in search of me, obviously worried. You can't fake that. I sometimes wonder if I could handle the truth behind that concern. It confirms for me that I'm someone she loves—but I'm also someone that she feels is vulnerable and needs protection.

Of course, she has her own take on our shared experience, and I'm sure she feels varying amounts of frustration, disappointment, and alarm. Our lives, and our happiness, require that we both be present and honest. As Tracy says, "Love is giving the benefit of the doubt." She's not always a rock, but that's okay. I always thought a rock was a silly metaphor for a supportive family member. Rocks are solid, stubborn, and immovable. That's me. Tracy, on the other hand, has learned to keep the rock rolling (apologies to Keith).

And so, on New Year's Day, 2018, we roll back to New York, four days earlier than planned.

9

WHAT TO EXPECT FROM MY BACK IN THE FUTURE

My first night back in Manhattan is spent under observation at Mount Sinai Hospital. I've convened my Parkinson's specialist, my neurologist, my internist, and even my cardiologist, to untie the Gordian knot that is my current health situation. The doctors agree that the sciatic pain is temporary, and that with a short period of rest, it will subside. I'm not buying it; this is Inquisition-grade agony. But after a quiet week at home, they'll be proven right. The other strands of the knot are more difficult to unwind. I have questions that need answers: Why are my limbs weak? Why are my fingers and toes numb? And why, as my hero Elvis Costello sings, can I not stand up for falling down? My propensity for falling—on my ass, face, and other body parts—is insidious.

A new MRI reveals the answer I had been dreading for a long time. The culprit, one unrelated to Parkinson's, is climbing up my spine.

You Can't Touch My Ependymoma

For years, my neurologist had been monitoring a growth in my spinal cord, an *ependymoma* tumor, which began in the ependymal cells that line the pathways for cerebrospinal fluid. The tumor first appeared on an MRI during an assessment of my neurofibromyalgia. At that time, I surveyed four differently affiliated surgeons, each of whom described the ependymoma as benign, but a serious concern, and laid out what would be involved in addressing the problem. The consensus was that I avoid invasive surgery to remove the mass. This would be an intensely complicated procedure; the work difficult, dangerous, and not likely to be 100 percent successful. They all agreed that the risks were prohibitive, and as long as the tumor was dormant and not overly compressing the spinal cord, the surgery was not advisable. "Let's wait, monitor it, and keep the focus on improving your PD therapy."

After remaining essentially static for years, things have taken a recent, ominous turn. Something has triggered an acceleration in the tumor's growth. And there's another red flag: The new imaging reveals a slight bleed in the cyst. This causes some rethinking of their "wait and see" position. Now these same doctors agree that the tumor should be removed.

Tracy and I consider all of this carefully. We're wary, even fearful, about the decision we have to make. We love our life, although after all of these years with Parkinson's, we know that few things are predictable. It's pretty clear now that this is more than just a pain in the ass; it is a tumor in my spine, and it's got to go. Now, the question is: Who's going to take it out, and when, and will they know what the hell they're doing?

The Northeast has some of the most prominent neurosurgeons in the country, at some of the most prestigious hospitals. We interview a number of them. They review the latest imaging, and weigh the risks inherent in attempting a fix. Some are willing; some hesitate; a few outright decline. I need a wise man or woman, to help us make a decision.

Dr. Allan H. Ropper, the legendary Harvard neurologist who guided me through the first years of my Parkinson's diagnosis, recommends that I meet with Dr. Nicholas Theodore, director of the Neurosurgical Spine Center at Johns Hopkins in Baltimore. Allan's son, Alexander E. Ropper, himself a neurosurgeon, worked as Dr. Theodore's fellow at his previous post at the Barrow Neurological Institute in Phoenix.

Tracy and I travel the I-95 from New York to Maryland to consult with Dr. Theodore. Nina is with us; in fact, Nina is driving. Johns Hopkins is an iconic institution, the birthplace of neurosurgery in the United States. Another reason to consider this hospital is their first-class and world-renowned rehabilitation facility, located in the same complex. I wouldn't have to transfer to a separate rehab location, post-surgery.

We reach the medical center and, once inside, I shuffle down a corridor toward a tall man in a white coat, waiting in a doorway, about twenty steps away. It seems more like twenty miles. Having difficulty with balance, I'm palming the wall for support. When we reach Dr. Theodore, he shows Tracy into a handsome office, and me into the adjoining exam room. It's the type of setup you'd expect for an acclaimed surgeon.

My first impression is that he's larger than life; a down-to-earth pro-linebacker with the demeanor of a happy John Goodman. Dr. Theodore says that he has reviewed my MRI several times, and is caught up on my medical history. He examines my spine, checks my reflexes, the regular drill. He records his observations into his computer: "Imaging shows a massive *intramedullary* [within the spinal cord] tumor, with a large, associated *syrinx* [a fluid-filled cavity within the cord] causing significant pressure. Deteriorating balance issues, significant weakness and spasticity in the legs, and clear-cut evidence of *myelopathy* [spinal cord dysfunction]."

As I am getting dressed, he comments on the cuts and scrapes on my knees. "Falling a lot?"

"Falling more and enjoying it less," I say.

"Do your knees ever get the chance to heal?"

"Not lately. I'm pretty rough on them."

We rejoin Tracy in Dr. Theodore's main office. He begins the meeting by explaining that when Dr. Ropper contacted him about a patient with an ependymoma in the upper thoracic spinal cord that no one else wanted to touch, it got his attention. Ropper chose not to reveal my identity until after Dr. Theodore agreed to consider my case. "When I first saw your imaging, I was alarmed, to say the least."

I glance at Tracy, who has pen in hand and is getting this all down in a spiral notebook.

"Any neurosurgeon," he continues, "would get a pit in their stomach, looking at your spine. I just had to take a deep breath." Dr. Theodore says he understands why others have shied away from this as being inoperable. "Given the size and location of the tumor at the cervicothoracic junction, it is risky." He then leans forward and confides, "I mean, who wants to be the guy who paralyzes Michael J. Fox?"

Most people don't evaluate neurosurgeons with a bias toward a sense of humor, but I tend to trust folks who make me laugh when things get grim. His last comment earns a chuckle from me.

Tracy speaks up. "Why do you think this growth initially started on his spine? We've heard differing opinions."

"We don't know why a tumor of this kind develops; whether he was born with the abnormal cells, or if it developed spontaneously. Either way, these types of tumors tend to grow slowly, so he may have had this for quite some time before he noticed he had a problem."

He turns from Tracy toward me. "In your case, Parkinson's disease probably made it difficult to detect a separate problem with your spine," he explains. "I don't need to tell you—PD is a progressive illness; it's constantly changing, so it would be easy to presume that the issues caused by the tumor were just new Parkinson's symptoms. It is highly unusual to have these two conditions simultaneously. I wouldn't want anyone to have either of them, let alone both."

"Well, my Parkinson's isn't going anywhere anytime soon. Knowing that, do you think you can fix the other problem?"

"There's definitely reason to hope that we can. But there are no guarantees or shortcuts." Dr. Theodore reviews the potential complications, including the possibility that I could experience worsened weakness, or, as other doctors feared, paralysis. "The blood supply in the thoracic spinal cord is very tenuous; it's minimal. A little too much manipulation, or a little blood vessel that goes into spasm, and the spinal cord decides it's not going to work anymore."

I listen carefully, but count on Tracy to absorb the details and ask all the right questions. In full advocate's mode, she asks, "Could you describe the procedure for us?"

"Of course. Assuming all goes well, the surgery will last about five hours. Once you are delivered to the OR, we'll prep you and put you to sleep. Then we'll turn you onto your belly and mark out the region of interest between your shoulder blades, where we are going to make our incision. We use ultrasound, your MRI, and other techniques to determine where to make the incision."

My nervousness fast approaching fear, I attempt to cut the tension. "Hey, at least it ain't brain surgery."

Dr. Theodore laughs. "I know you've actually had brain surgery, but that's much easier than what we're talking about."

Tracy adds, "Mike's brain surgeon said the same thing about his job versus a rocket scientist."

No Margin for Error

In 1998, I had a *thalamotomy*, the destruction of specific cells in the part of the brain called the thalamus that controls involuntary movement.

Dr. Bruce Cook, the neurosurgeon in charge, drilled a hole through my skull and fed a filament down through the brain to the target. He explained why, in the age-old comparison between rocket scientists and brain surgeons, surgeons prevail: There's no margin for error. "We've all seen *Apollo 13*," he said. "If something goes wrong, they can always go to plastic bags, cardboard, and duct tape. Brain surgeons are on the phone to find a good malpractice lawyer."

Dr. Theodore offers his own comparison: "If I was operating on your brain, I could touch it with a probe. We don't have that ability with the spinal cord. We can't navigate it in the same way. Instead, we use your MRI like a map. In my mind, I have to superimpose the MRI onto the cord to build a 3D model, so I can determine where the tumor is located."

"You don't actually make an incision into the spinal cord, though?" Tracy queries.

"That's a good question. Yes, but we begin by cutting into the membrane around the cord, called the *dura mater*, Latin for 'tough mother.' It's a white, fibrous sheath, like Gore-Tex, that keeps in the spinal fluid. The fluid acts as a buffer for your brain and spinal cord. We then make a linear incision into the spinal cord's outer layer, exposing fibers that run up and down. Then we spread those fibers, very gently, like a beaded curtain."

Okay, now I've officially hit fear. *Who is this spinal cracker, anyway? Am I going to let him do this to me?* I'm feeling slightly dizzy, and I don't want to let on to Tracy and Dr. Theodore that I'm freaking out a little. My eyes focus on the standard collection of diplomas, spread across the wall behind the doctor's desk. Med school: Georgetown. Residency: Bethesda Naval Hospital and the Barrow Neurological Institute. A fellowship at the Neuroscience Division at the NIH.

Slacker!

He has my attention again, as he continues to describe the surgery. "We carefully spread the fibers in the cord, until we find the tumor. Once we open it up and look at it under a microscope, we can start to define the extent of the tumor, and its aspects. Next we'll need to determine how 'stuck' it is, and figure out where the fluid comes into play. When I am satisfied with the data collected, I will begin to meticulously scrape off the tumor. I'll take my time—millimeter by millimeter—to peel it away from your spine."

Tracy looks up from her notebook. Insightful, intelligent, and a recovering hypochondriac, my wife is a savant when it comes to all things medical. She knows exactly how to drill down to the core issues. "I get the purpose, and I think I get the process. But in plain terms, what does success look like?"

"Success means there will be no further progression," Dr. Theodore answers. He is confident, but frank. He meets my gaze and assures me, "I believe in my heart that I can help you. But understand, the goal is not to fix anything that has already been damaged—that will be impossible. Serious balance issues will persist, and there is no cure for the cramping in your quads and the numbness on the back of your legs. And as a result of the surgery, more than the tumor itself, for a period of time your challenges around walking will remain, or perhaps even worsen."

Sounds like a shit salad. Maybe I'll pass. "And what happens if I decide not to risk surgery?"

"You're deteriorating. Without surgery, things probably won't go well. In my experience—looking at your symptoms and your films—in a short period of time, you'd be left unable to walk."

Tracy slips her hand into mine.

"I realize this is not an easy decision," Dr. Theodore acknowledges. "The journey is going to be difficult. A lot of what you will feel in the weeks and months after the procedure will be your body's reaction to the intrusion of the surgery. But gradually, you'll feel better, as the pain and discomfort subside."

He pauses. "Mike, any questions?"

I look at Tracy. "Honey, what do you think? Do you want to go somewhere and talk about it?"

"How do *you* feel?" she asks quietly.

"Me? Like dura mater." Off her look, "I'm a tough mother."

"Yes, you are," she says with a soft smile.

I make the decision, right then. "We're going to go through with it."

Nina comes in and talks to the doctor about logistics, and we all agree on a surgical date. From now on, she will coordinate and troubleshoot. Nina is a combination of fierce efficiency and good-natured affability; so integral to my day-to-day existence, I refer to her as "my frontal lobe." Pausing for a moment, she turns to make a quick, discreet transaction between us. From her bag she produces a small Altoids canister and pops it open with a practiced thumb. I take two tablets. "I knew right then she was good," Dr. Theodore tells me later. "She intuited that you wanted a mint, from across the room."

"Actually, it was a mix of PD meds," I explain. "She could tell I needed some before I even started to tremor." Nina is my Radar O'Reilly. Her uncanny ability to anticipate whatever is required is just one reason why she's so invaluable.

In less than a week, we all return to Johns Hopkins. Having resolved to proceed, there is no time to waste. Each day's losses cannot be reclaimed.

10

SHOWING SOME SPINE

Ready for my close-up. The surgery is tomorrow, but today I'm on a gurney, in a hospital gown, and hooked up to an IV that is dripping sedative. I'm being delivered not to the operating room, but to radiology. Part of Dr. Theodore's strategy in dealing with the Parkinson's/spinal cord duality, is that he must have a pristine MRI to work from. This is the map of my spine he'll rely on so heavily. The image needs to be as crisp as possible; no PD symptoms, no movement whatsoever. For that to be possible, I must be unconscious. I'm given just enough drug to keep me knocked out until Theodore has his pictures of my back (my best side).

The rest of the day I spend in my hospital room with a slight headache, while Nina negotiates with the hospital's administrators about who will dispense my Parkinson's medications during and after the surgery. This is a big deal, because you can't self-medicate in a hospital; they have to account for every pill I take. Every drug, compound, and medicine must be checked for contraindication.

Tracy is in the room with me. We're both quiet, I suppose each for our own reasons. I try to nap; my eyes close, but my brain won't stop. I'm thinking about twenty years earlier. In Boston for my brain surgery, Tracy was frightened, visibly nervous, while I was completely unfazed. I knew the risk, but I also knew the reward: relief from the severe tremors wracking the left side of my body, inhibiting my family, work, and social life. I just wanted to be able to hold a book and read to my kids. I didn't obsess about the outcome; I felt sure the surgery would be a success.

My primary concern was helping Tracy understand that.

That was in 1998, when we'd been married for ten years. Do wedding vows still say "in sickness and in health"? Well, ours did, and with my Parkinson's diagnosis, I cashed that check. I still work this reality through my head and my heart. Twenty years later, now married for thirty years, Tracy has been healthy; I've been the only beneficiary of that clause in the contract. In sickness and in health—that's us. I know which of the two I've been, but I believe it's still possible that I can be both.

I am particularly sensitive to the extra strain I might be placing on Tracy, because as present and caring as she is for me through this ordeal, I know she is also thinking of her father. Stephen Pollan passed away a few months ago. He was eighty-nine when he died. Stephen possessed a wisdom commensurate with his age, but had a ten-year-old's appetite for mischief.

One Sunday afternoon at their farmhouse in Connecticut, Stephen was sitting alone at the kitchen table, his regular perch. A big man, warm and disarming, in a cardigan sweater over a button-down flannel, he'd always wear a baseball cap on the weekends; not so much *wear,* as allow to surf atop a silver wave of hair. He sported a white beard in the style of C. Everett Koop. He had the *Times* laid out in front of him, and was reading the business pages. I picked up the sports section and took a seat. I was checking the Yankees' box scores, and a casual conversation ensued. It was unusual for Stephen to discuss my health issues; we both just found more interesting things to talk about. But on this day, he put down his paper, slid his glasses up onto the bridge of his nose, and said, "So, how are you doing?"

"All things considered, I'm doing okay. How about you?"

"Good. How's Tracy?"

"She's great. But that's what I wanted to talk to you about."

He sat back and folded his hands on the tabletop. "Shoot."

"The day we got married, and the minister—or was it the rabbi?—one of them said, 'In sickness and in health . . .' I don't think Tracy expected the 'sickness' part quite so soon."

I put my elbow on the table and rested my head on the palm of my hand. "Sometimes I worry it's unfair to her. She didn't sign up for this."

He pondered for a beat, and then, "Look, kiddo. Yes, she did. Tracy is a very strong, very devoted person. You both just have to take it one day at a time. I don't know about sickness and health, but I gotta say, you did okay on the *for richer or for poorer* part."

That was funny, and I appreciated it coming from my father-in-law. But to know Stephen was to know that he was offering much more than a quip about money. He was observing that my life with Tracy is rich in a much more tangible, soulful, and loving way, and we are both responsible for that wealth.

With these thoughts, I drift in and out of a nap in my room at Johns Hopkins. At some point, I take a peek at Tracy, sitting by the window in a plastic chair. She has waited for me in that chair, or versions of it, during so many consultations and medical tests and procedures. It occurs to me now: She wants to be here for me, in sickness or in health.

The A-Team

It's 7:00 a.m. We are in the pre-op staging area. Tracy and I share a good-bye kiss; well, not *goodbye*—a see-you-later kiss. Tracy tells me that once they put me out, it will seem like only a second until I wake up, and she'll be there again. In the meantime, she joins Nina in the family lounge, where they'll wait, worry, make phone calls to update family and friends, and in Tracy's case, use the downtime to rock the Candy Crush. Alex, one of Dr. Theodore's associates, will provide progress reports during the surgery.

I'm wheeled into the operating room. Strangers in scrubs, surgical masks, and hospital-issue Crocs, like pale green ghosts, float around the table. Conferring in mumbles, they point their heads toward me and mutter some more. It hits me: *I'm here. I'm actually doing this.* Why *am I doing this? Is the surgery going to work, or is my spine ultimately beyond repair? What if this turns out to be an express ticket to where I was going to end up anyway?*

I've been so positive, so optimistic. The magnitude of the risk I am taking will reveal whether optimism is truly a friend in a foxhole. Will that quality endure, will it sustain me? I'd always believed so, but in the months ahead, my optimism will be put on trial.

Dr. Theodore strides in. If he's at all nervous about the next five to six hours, he doesn't let on. I turn to him for reassurance, and he delivers it with full force. Laying a hand on my shoulder, he says, "Good morning, Mike. Let me introduce you to everybody. This," he says, with a sweeping gesture toward the gathered phantoms, "is the A-team. All from the deep end of the pool—all highly skilled specialists." He introduces me to the nurses, chosen in consultation with the director of nursing. "And I think you've met my fellow, Corinna Zygourakis. She's brilliant—an excellent surgeon," he says. "She'll be with me the whole time." Dr. Zygourakis smiles, then turns back to her prep. Another green-clad figure approaches: "Hello, Mr. Fox. I'm Dr. Gottschalk. I'll be overseeing your pain and sleep meds."

"Allan is our chief of neuroanesthesia—he's unflappable and extremely bright. A rock star." I think, *Well, rock stars do know their drugs.*

Gottschalk pats my arm. "You won't feel a thing, I promise."

Dr. Theodore leans in a little closer now, and says, "It's like Fantasy Football, Mike. I picked the best of the best."

These faces, no longer entirely strange to me, happy in their work, go about their final ministrations. Dr. Gottschalk dispenses a preliminary dose of sedative. As I begin to drift off, I take one more glance at the A-team, believing they'll do their best. I wish them luck.

Slip Slidin' Away

Transferred post-surgery to the Neurocritical Care Unit, I begin the torpid reemergence from the anesthesia, and sample small bites of consciousness. Through heavy eyelids, I see a soft-focus Tracy; by her side, Schuyler. I'm too addled to react. As Tracy promised, it seems like mere seconds ago that we were last together.

If any of us imagined we'd be high-fiving each other in the afterglow of victory, we were mistaken. The room is quiet, except for the hushed tones and muted movements of the hospital staff. Tracy bends toward me and whispers, "Dr. Theodore says it went well, really well. He couldn't be happier."

But this is the calm before the storm, soon to escalate into a combination of *The Snake Pit* and *A Beautiful Mind*. Gradually, my behavior starts to change. To Tracy, I seem "level-headed" in a matter-of-fact way, looking right at her and saying, "I'm fine." But over the next few hours, we begin dealing with a new reality, or *sur*reality. My grasp on where I am and who I am becomes tenuous. For our daughter Sky—a recent graduate of a liberal arts college with a degree in psychology—it is traumatizing, a crash course in semi-madness.

The triggering event: Two orderlies transfer me into a railed bed. I cannot feel my legs or my back, so I don't feel secure. I can't feel my body's weight pushing against the surface of the bed. I have a very real sensation of sliding. A slight panic ensues. I start sputtering in a rising voice, "I'm slipping off the bed. I'm falling!" The staff's reassuring (*condescending?*) smiles piss me off. I urgently insist that they are trying to spill me from the bed and onto the hospital tiles. Tracy and Sky grow alarmed, and ask if there's anything that can be done. I overhear parts of the explanation offered by a nurse.

Apparently, I had been administered an unusually generous allowance of anesthetic over two successive days. There was yesterday's dose to ensure a perfect MRI; light but effective in knocking me out. And then, less than twenty-four hours later, a more substantial round to prepare for surgery. Mid-procedure, another dose had been required. Added to the cocktail, an opiate analgesic for pain management, plus a medley of my regular PD meds, and the end result is one spaced cowboy.

In my druggy haze, I'm convinced that there's a conspiracy to injure and humiliate me. I am sure that the hospital has lured me here under false pretenses. I shout at the medical team, "You were supposed to fix me, but I can't feel my back, I can't feel my legs! You're not doctors; you're actors. You're tricking me! I know—I'm an actor, too." And here come the threats: "You're going to get a call from my lawyer, Cliff. *He's my lawyer.* Cliff will get me out of here!" (Cliff, an even-keeled entertainment lawyer who handles contracts and profit participation, would want no part of this.)

The evening brings a segue into a more mild-mannered lunacy, filled with hallucinations and delusions. I am surrounded by illegible graffiti and animated cartoon characters; icons and avatars inscribed on the ether between my eyes and the nearest wall. I complain to Tracy about my hands of straw, from which I keep trying to extract little bits of reedy grass, stalk by imaginary stalk. I can't get rid of the straw (because it's not really there). Suddenly alarmed, I warn Sky about a silverback gorilla lurking in the corner of the room; she turns to see a rumpled overcoat, draped on a chair. "It's a silverback," I insist. Tracy reacts to me with empathy. "We don't see a gorilla there, honey, but we can understand that you do, and that must be so scary for you."

Damn right, the gorilla *is* scary, and he's on the move among the medical staff, who look like regulars at the *Star Wars* cantina. A man visiting another patient brandishes what is likely a cell phone, but looks to me like a camera. I point it out to Tracy, who smiles gently and touches my hair. "Don't worry, he's not taking your picture."

"You're right," I agree. "I think he's taking a picture of the monster." I gesture toward an empty space at the foot of the bed. "It's waiting for me to slide down there."

I have few memories of any of this, beyond Tracy and Sky's recounting. The nurses later add their own accounts, but they assure me that it was just another day at the office; nothing they hadn't seen before.

My wife and daughter know that this crazy person they're seeing and hearing isn't normal. Tracy, though upset, understands what is happening, but Sky is quite disturbed by the sight of her normally amiable *Dood* possessed by a ranting stranger. Tracy reassures her that it is temporary, and will eventually pass. Schuyler, the psychologist, is not as confident.

Babies in the Windows

I am feeling much better by day three. Tracy, Sky, and Nina are with me in the NCCU. My daughter sits beside my bed, holding my hand and playing classical music for me on her iPhone. Tracy helps me relax by coaching me through deep-breathing exercises. Nina is across the room, making phone calls. After a while, Sky ditches the classical tunes for an oldies rock playlist, stuff she learned from me: the Doobie Brothers, Joe Walsh, Led Zeppelin. "There you go, Dood. Rock on with your bad self."

Sky tosses her backpack onto the windowsill. I subtly nod at Tracy, point to it, and whisper, "Gorilla." Faces fall, and everyone fixes me with sad stares.

"Just kidding. I know it's a backpack."

Tracy's eyes narrow. "Mike. That's not funny."

Sky concurs. "Too soon, Dad."

Nina walks over, pocketing her cell phone. "Sky, do you want to hit the vending machines?" Tracy watches them go.

"I think Sky's uncomfortable with this," she says, worried.

"Yeah, but she's not leaving," I say. "She didn't take her gorilla."

Tracy laughs. "I'll admit, it's good to see you more like yourself today. Even if yourself is a jerk."

"Yeah, I'll apologize to her. That was kind of shitty."

It's quiet again. Together, Tracy and I take in the view out the window, a courtyard overlooking the oldest part of the hospital. Rows of nineteenth-century casements line the brick facade. In each window, I'm sure that I see a smiling baby, tiny hands spread-fingered and pressed against the glass. "Tra, look at all the babies." I point from my bed. "There are babies in the windows."

Tracy knows me too well to mistake this for a joke. Her silent answer: She calmly closes the shade. I still have a long way to go.

11

METAPHYSICAL THERAPY

An old movie cliché that I always found particularly tedious is the one in which a patient, convinced there's nothing wrong with him, attempts to escape the hospital. The nurse steps out of his room for a minute, and he leaps from his bed, pulls the tubes out of his nose, and reaches into the closet for his raincoat, which he drapes over his hospital gown. He slides into his shoes, slaps a hat on his head, and bolts for the exit. *Who does that?* Movie characters. The cranky patient, who badgers and frustrates the hospital staff. He's annoying, self-centered, and second-guesses every diagnosis or recommendation.

During the two weeks I spend in the Johns Hopkins Medical Center following surgery, I am that guy. I am "His Majesty, the Baby." The staff can't do enough for me. Once moved out of Critical Care and into the rehab wing, I straighten up my act somewhat and I am a little more civil. The truth is, I can't just flee the building. Not for lack of will; I simply can't walk.

Two staffers check me out of the NCCU and transfer me into a wheelchair. It feels strange to be out of that bed. Over the past few days, it has been everything from a life raft, to a flying carpet, to a hamster cage. I say goodbye and apologize to the medical team in the ward; they are gracious, and actually have nice things to say. Rolling away, I look over my shoulder to be sure the bed isn't following.

The trip to the rehab wing, the Acute Inpatient Rehabilitation Unit, seems to take forever. Rolling down hallways the length of football fields, through fire doors, across vestibules, and in and out of elevators, I am quiet and try not to be too concerned that I can't feel my feet. I'm not sure what I'd do with them if I could. Is this chair going to be my permanent ride?

We slow down and take a sharp left into a spacious room with a much friendlier hospital bed in the center, and a bitchin' oversized recliner near the window. My first impression is that I'm checking into a decent, three-star airport hotel room. A quick tour: They wheel me over to the bathroom door, through which I can see a wheelchair-accessible shower, a low metal toilet, and a sink. I'll be bouncing out of this joint in no time.

It's not that I dislike the hospital or the staff, or that I have any particular complaint at all; at least, once I become compos mentis. I simply lack the patience for healing. I yearn to slip that overcoat on, throw on the hat, and make like a tree. But I am also pragmatic enough to understand that I can't leave without physical rehabilitation. If I can't get better over the next week or so, I'll at least *look* like I'm better. Short of becoming stable, my personal mission is to use my acting skills to appear stable. I intend to recover at a miraculous rate; zip through treatment, master all of the challenges, do a dance on Dr. Theodore's desk, and get the hell back to New York. Unfortunately, I just had spinal surgery, and I can't do any of that.

Tracy brings in dinner from a local Indian restaurant, and we enjoy it together in the mega-recliner. I say good night to my wife, and to Nina, who is always nearby. I dim the lights and watch a little play-off hockey before they hand out the nighttime meds. In what has become a routine, I pull the bottom of the sheets and blankets up past my ankles, so that I can keep track of my feet. They get up to some strange things in the night.

Defy, Not Comply

The next morning, I ask if I can shower. The nurse sets me up with a couple of towels and a bath chair, which she walks me to. I remove my gown as she turns on the water. It's the first shower I've had in days. The wound is dressed and safely sealed in plastic, so I'm free to let the warm, soothing water run down my back. I reach for the soap and the nurse hands it to me; I realize in that moment that she's my new shower pal. She's not going anywhere, and neither am I.

Short of escape, I test the limits. As with the shower, I am observed and attended to almost constantly—but in the rare unobserved moments, I slip out of bed or the recliner or whatever safe place I am nesting in, and try to take a few tentative steps. Like a tightrope walker in army boots, I stumble forward and then back. Feeble and unsteady, I fall against the bed's soft surface. These unauthorized sorties are a bad idea. Still, I feel like I'm getting away with something. My first inclination is to defy, when it should be to comply. Time will reveal how idiotic and shortsighted this was.

For the first time since I moved into the rehab wing, Dr. Theodore stops by for a visit, ostensibly to fill me in on the post-surgical game plan. But word of my Bambi-ish perambulations has reached him, and he is none too pleased. After a pleasant inquiry into how I'm feeling, comes a reprimand. "I hear you're trying to walk on your own already."

"Yeah, just checking out the wheels."

The next word from Dr. Theodore is surprisingly abrupt. "Stop." He never raises his voice, but remains stern. "I can't overemphasize the delicacy of the work we've done on your spine; the fragility of it. If you keep screwing around, you're going to fall, and then I can't help you. I won't be able to fix it. It won't just be a skinned knee; it may be a reversal of everything that we've done. It may be paralysis."

I find that my spine is still capable of registering a chill.

"Let me explain again what we did to you in there. I know I went through the basics of the procedure, but you need to understand that each step represented a potential disaster."

He has my attention, even if I don't want to hear it.

"Usually, when we open up the dura to inspect the spinal cord, there's a spontaneous gush of fluid; in your case, there wasn't any. Your cord was so swollen, there was no fluid to gush. And normally with each heartbeat, the spinal cord pulsates, but that wasn't happening, either. The tumor was strangling your cord."

I let that settle in.

"We had to carefully incise the back of the spinal cord, and the tumor slowly started to come out under significant pressure, like squeezing a tube of toothpaste. But part of the tumor started to ooze out spontaneously, without anyone squeezing."

This is a lot more graphic than the scenario he laid out for Tracy and me in his office: "pulsating," "squeezing," "oozing," "strangling."

"Are those words part of the normal surgical lexicon, or was mine a special case?"

"Well, put it this way," he confides. "I had to switch into Zen mode. For five hours, every fiber of my being was focused on your spine. You know, the cord is only about the size of your pinky finger, and it doesn't appreciate being manipulated. For your surgery, I had asked my mentor to design specialized dissection tools, and using an ultrasonic aspiration device, I removed the tumor still remaining within the cord. As soon as the pressure was relieved, the spinal cord began to pulsate again, like it was supposed to."

I'm speechless. This is this guy's job.

"It was a meticulous resection—I had to carefully inspect every nook and cranny of the tumor cavity to make sure it was all removed."

It's clear that he felt a deep sense of mental relief, getting that tumor out.

"But we weren't celebrating yet. Every neurosurgeon will tell you about the time it all went great, but then the patient woke up . . ."

"In bad shape?"

He considers that and after a beat, rephrases it. "With a neurological deficit."

"When did you know I was okay? I am okay, right?"

He nods and takes a seat on the edge of the bed, across from my position at the helm of the *Starship Lounger*.

"I saw you when you were first waking up from surgery, before I spoke with Tracy. I asked you to wiggle your toes and lift your legs. Your leg strength was impressive, especially in light of what you'd just gone through. You lifted your legs off the bed." He says this with such a smile that I feel compelled to do it for him again. Seems easy enough. "You see, that's beautiful. If I had a football, I'd spike it. The surgery could have left your spinal cord stunned, but your strength is nearly perfect."

"Well," I say, "I like to start out perfect and improve from there."

He stands to leave. "But remember, while it's wonderful that you have strength in your legs, it doesn't mean you're going to be able to use them right away. Basically, you'll have to learn to walk again, but this shows me that you have the strength to do that. So, tomorrow we start therapy. Ten days. I'll check in with you in the morning."

I realize how much this means to him—how much I mean to him as a patient—and I want to honor that. I understand, too, that it will be disastrous for both of us if I do anything foolish or selfish to undo this work.

His exit line is emphatic: "Just don't fall. Please. Don't fall."

In case Dr. Theodore's bedside chat doesn't get the message across, the hospital's approach is more direct. *Minimize risk.* Allowing me to take risks is too big a risk for them to take. It becomes the staff's priority to watch me like a hawk; they must protect me from myself. I discover, upon waking up in the middle of the night, that an alarm has been installed on my bed. I've already been accessorized with a bracelet in Day-Glo orange that designates me a "Fall Risk." Those two words are meant to be cautionary and instructive, but my first reaction is to feel shamed and stigmatized. What's next, a bell around my neck?

What they don't understand, and I can't convey, is that it's not just my restless spirit that prompts my night wandering. It's the Parkinson's. Sometimes it demands that I move my legs; it's like Restless Leg Syndrome on steroids. Or quite possibly, the hospital staff do understand this, but it simply can't be helped. I must not get up and walk around, unsupervised, or I will fall.

Risky Business

I think about how and why I got here. I had been given a choice: Do I have this surgery, or decline and hope for the best? Either choice would have consequences. It all came down to my capacity for risk, and I'd rather take a risk by being proactive, attempting to shape the result.

One man's passivity is another man's resignation. I had to take the chance.

Risk is a part of who I am; it is encoded in my DNA. Teenagers lack a fully formed prefrontal cortex; they can't reliably assess risk. I was the poster boy for this developmental delay. Anxious to prove that my physical stature was not reflective of my intestinal fortitude, I was game for anything. In my teens, I engaged in reckless activities (I didn't consider them risks), and sought adventures—diversions that could have easily resulted in failure, bodily injury, and quite possibly, premature death. But I wasn't thinking about any of that.

In the bodily injury department: I played box lacrosse in the '70s, a version of the grueling sport invented by the Native Americans of the Northeast. Interestingly, lacrosse is Canada's national sport, not hockey, as one
would assume. Unlike collegiate lacrosse—played on an open, grassy field
with plastic sticks, and governed by rules about contact—box lacrosse is a
blood sport, even for thirteen-year-olds. The "box," an off-season hockey
rink (indoors or out) with a concrete surface instead of ice, is surrounded
by hardboards which your opponent slams you into, usually with a cross-
check to the kidneys. The sticks we wielded were inverted canes made of
hickory, with baskets of catgut and leather.

I played for a couple of seasons. My first year, I was assigned to the
"C" league: essentially, a beginner's league. I played quite well, and
scored a few goals, more than anyone expected. The next year, I was
drafted into the "A" league, leap-frogging the "B's" to the top level.
This was an error. I remember the locker room on the first day: I put
on my gear, looked around, and noticed two things about the rest of my
team. Number one, they wanted nothing to do with me. Two, these were
thirteen-year-old men, average height: 6' 4", and they *shaved*. They had
chest hair and enormous feet. I was 5' 1", and 110 pounds in full pads and
a helmet. Even the coaches who drafted me were wearing expressions of
doubt and regret.

I played great at first; fast, elusive, and able to put the rock-hard Indian
rubber ball behind the goaltender and into the net. And then I got hit. I was
slow to get up. My parents noticed this, with some alarm.

After the next few games, my mom said, "You still like playing lacrosse?"

"Yeah, I love it, Mom."

"It seems a lot rougher than it used to be. You get hurt more often."

"I don't get hurt."

"I'm having a tough time washing the blood out of your sweater."

My parents suggested I move down to the "B's," where I'd be safer. I
declined, stayed in the "A's," got my ass kicked, and learned to deal with

it. Although, when invited to play in the "B" league the following year, I chose retirement instead.

The seminal risk of my young life was to leave school in the eleventh grade, with a vague notion—it didn't even rise to the level of a plan—to go to Los Angeles and embark on an acting career. Having performed in a few local TV and theater productions, I would have been confused by the suggestion that I was taking a risk. To me, it was more of a gamble to stay in Canada. That is not meant to disparage my country or my family, but I thought there was something else out there for me. By sitting in a classroom, I risked not being there to meet it.

It's not that I lacked the willingness to learn; I just rejected the structured type of learning that relied on traditional guidelines. If I failed to write a paper that was due in history, it would be uncomfortable for a while, but then I'd be on to the next paper I didn't do. I'd explain to my teacher, "Look, I know all about the Marshall Plan and the reorganization of Europe; I'd just rather not write a paper about it. We can stay here for a half an hour, and I'll run through it for you." School had become the worst of all possible situations: One that offered neither risk nor reward.

Obviously, people in my life, my parents most of all, questioned my decision to leave school, home, and country for an acting career. It seemed like an insane proposition. They considered me naive, overconfident, short-sighted, and reckless; a cautionary tale waiting to happen. I was all of those things. But I saw this gambit not as a means to an end, but a means to a means. I needed to put myself in a place where I could get on with the rest of my life. I could go be an actor, a thing I loved to do, and work with great words and stories and interesting people, and maybe even be affirmed for doing it.

If you don't take risks, there's no room for luck. I took a chance. I got lucky.

Whac-a-Mole

I envision a movie montage. An '80s "hair band" power ballad thumps in the background. Open on a close-up: me, mid-surgery. In a rapid series of vignettes: Dr. Theodore and his A-team tear into me; instruments are passed to Dr. T, and a nurse blots his beaded brow; the flash of a scalpel; blood and extraneous fluids gush out and spray his mask and safety goggles. Then, close-up on me, post-op, reacting to the news: *Success!* Next, a time lapse of me mastering physical therapy, crushing it—walking on the apparatus with the handrails, then without the handrails; quickly gaining strength; and soon, running on the beach. The *Rocky*-esque theme swells as I arrive home through my front door, upright and fully recovered, swarmed by my adoring family and a tail-wagging Gus, the Wonder Dog.

Nope. That isn't happening.

My first physiotherapy session: I'm attempting something new—using a walker. It's a battle, and the walker is winning. My upper body wants to push the contraption forward at a faster rate than my barely responsive legs can attain. I end up in a suspended push-up position, with no leverage; a sensation like having your toes on one side of an opening drawbridge and your hands on another.

Johns Hopkins has an impressive rehab facility, a large gymnasium-like room outfitted with equipment and apparatus, from foosball to animatronic walking suits, canes, balance beams, and parallel bars. Supporting myself with one hand on the walker, my feet tenuously balanced inside the frame, I am playing an ersatz game of volleyball with my PT, Erik. He's a tremendously fit guy with a low-key, take-it-as-it-comes style. I'm able to consistently return the bouncy beach ball; I like this walker much better when I'm not moving in it. During the back-and-forth with the ball, the walker is just a rail to hold on to.

At some point, mid-volley, Dr. Theodore enters the facility. Taking in the spectacle of my wobbly efforts, he is giddy. "Karch Kiraly!" he calls out, referring to the accomplished beach volleyball player. Distracted, I whiff at the next return and nearly topple forward over the walker's bars.

So much for the easy stuff. Dr. T wants to see the gamut. Joined by an associate, they observe as Erik puts me through a series of core exercises, tests of balance, and repetitions on small sets of stairs with the support of guide rails, all requiring simple, coordinated locomotion. Baby steps. At the end of the session, we go to an adjacent hospital corridor, half the length of a football field. Closely tended by Erik, I somehow make my shaky way to the end and back in my new frenemy, the walker. The problem is, my feet can't keep up.

"Stay inside the frame," they keep telling me, but as Parkinson's only amplifies, my brain and my body are barely on speaking terms. This will prove to be a lasting issue. That's the exhausting part. Every movement, every command, everything that should be reflex, is a negotiation between Donald Trump and Nancy Pelosi (I don't have to tell you which one is the brain).

It is a demanding morning of intense therapy, challenging my strength and stamina. I feel a strain in every muscle and fiber of my body. From the reaction of the doctor, Erik, and the staff, I am ahead of projections and exceeding expectations. My rehab at Johns Hopkins begins a pattern of steady improvement that will carry on with a new set of therapists next month, back in New York.

Occupational Hazard

"Let's focus on how to open a cabinet safely," the occupational therapist suggests. It's the afternoon of the first day, and I'm here to work on a different facet of my rehabilitation. Standing inside the frame of my walker, I can't help myself: "Does it really take that much focus?" Over the course of my OT sessions at Johns Hopkins, I learn best practices for myriad banal, everyday tasks, a lot of them having to do with simple household chores: loading the dishwasher, carrying laundry, setting the oven temperature correctly. Tracy finds this hilarious. "He won't be doing any of this stuff," she laughs. "You'd have an easier time getting a photo of Bigfoot than one of Michael loading a dishwasher."

Tracy is with me for these early sessions, and so is Sam. Schuyler has returned to New York City for work, and my son has arrived in Maryland to tag in and join Tracy. Originally scheduled to visit later in the week, Sam pushed his schedule ahead when Tracy and Sky shared with him the highlights of my post-op derangement. By the time he gets here, I have recovered my mind, and am now preparing to reclaim my body.

I didn't anticipate the mental exhaustion and frustration of the occupational therapy piece. Truth is, basic manipulation of objects—performance of rituals such as dressing, putting on socks, retrieving a jar from a shelf using a "grabber" doohickey—probably address deficiencies related more to my Parkinson's than to my surgery.

Though Sam is here for the morning session to witness my first attempts at walking—where he is very good at making me laugh and short-circuiting my tendency to get frustrated and overexert—it is during the occupational therapy in the afternoon that he becomes part of the process. After the socks and the cabinets, we move on to coordination and reflex exercises. These take the form of games like Whac-a-Mole, flash cards, and brainteasers. Sandra, my OT, asks me if I've ever tried Wii bowling. I say I can't remember having played it. Sam corrects me.

"Yeah, we gave it to Grammy a few years ago for Christmas. We played it a few times."

"Was I good?"

"No," Sam says. "You sucked, actually."

I play Sam. We agree on the best two out of three. The third game isn't necessary; he destroys me.

"Well, given the physical circumstances, it's not exactly fair, or even," I complain, putting my imaginary bowling ball back in the virtual rack.

Sam said, "You're right, Pops. I'm taller than you."

With that, my son slips easily past the hard truth: I had been flailing like a blindfolded duck. Not only that; I'm at a loss for how this will prepare me for life with PD and a bad back.

I had expected that therapy would be brutal, challenging, painful; and it is. But I do have support. I love my family; I love their concern, their affection, their presence. I'm grateful to, and impressed by, the doctors, therapists, and staff. I feel them wanting a positive outcome so badly for me. But what I'm only now starting to fully understand is that this is an inside job. It only works if *I* believe. I've always been confident, positive, doggedly determined; but doubt is beginning to mitigate my conviction. Who am I to think I can accomplish this, when so many have struggled with similar setbacks; some with Parkinson's, some with the aftermath of spinal surgery? I may be the only one who has taken on this particular two-headed beast.

12

WALK THIS WAY

I put in ten days of rehab at Johns Hopkins. Honest about the rigors of this process, my physical therapist, Erik, encouraged me to be clear-eyed about my prospects. We didn't always agree on methods; to my chagrin, he insisted that the walker was the immediate solution. I still found it difficult to use. It felt strange and awkward, low-tech yet baffling. Moreover, I was embarrassed. Elderly people use walkers all the time. Most seem efficient with them—they clip along with their tennis balls and all-weather wheels—but I had a problem making it down a hospital corridor without slipping into the plank position.

So, I resisted the walker and tried a cane, but with little satisfaction. Though a simple, archaic device, the cane required a rhythm that didn't feel natural to me. Cane in right hand, moving forward with the left foot, immediately after which I attempted to follow with the right. When assisted, I could manage eight or ten halting steps before becoming exhausted. Sometimes, I'd be agitated to the point of tremoring; frozen in place, unsteady on my legs, tapping out Morse code with my cane, a bad actor playing Ebenezer Scrooge in *A Christmas Carol*. Erik's regimen was intensive, but he was committed to helping me improve, and acknowledged every accomplishment.

In addition to PT, I had two sessions of occupational therapy each day to continue regaining my soft skills. A third member of the Johns Hopkins team, Melissa, a therapeutic recreational specialist, was charged with assessing my mental acuity. She focused on elementary cognitive work, exercises like matching squares on a game board, meant to test memorization and reaction time. It was child's play for a fifty-six-year-old man, and I cringed when my therapist applauded a correct response. *Jesus. If this is what success looks like, I have a long way to go.*

The Manhattan Project

On the day of my release, I do not make that dramatic film noir exit from the hospital, storming out with my hat and overcoat and jumping into a cab. Instead, I go meekly, in a wheelchair, wearing sweatpants and a puffy coat. Tracy had rented a van for Nina to drive us back to New York; unfortunately, what arrives from the rental company is an enormous, airport-style bus. How is Nina supposed to drive this monstrosity? She would need a different class of operator's license for such a gas-guzzling lane hog. Our own SUV, in which Nina had delivered us to Baltimore, is no Mini Cooper, but it won't fit all of us. After some discussion, we decide that Tracy, Nina, Emily (my health aide), and I will pack into the SUV. Sam, soldier that he is, offers to take Amtrak home to Gotham.

I am quiet for much of the trip, feeling that I have many things to sort out. Still, I am optimistic. I'm going home—our giant bed, my giant dog, midnight fridge raids, and of course, time with my family, who have visited the hospital in one- or two-at-a-time combinations. I'm anxious to see them all at the same time.

Back in Manhattan, Tracy and Nina unload the car while I'm rolled into our building to find Esmé waiting for me in the lobby. I haven't seen her in three weeks. Being a sophomore in high school, homework and other commitments prevented her from visiting the hospital in Maryland. She's not sure how to approach me, other than gently, so she leans in with a soft hug. I notice that the doormen, Sonny and Danny, have placed a temporary wheelchair ramp over the two short flights of stairs leading to the elevator.

I turn to Esmé and ask, "Who in the building has a wheelchair?"

She pauses for a second, and then, with a slight tilt of her head, "Um . . . You?"

My daughter takes my hand as I'm wheeled into the elevator. When the door opens onto the foyer of our apartment, she says, "I know you can't smell them, but I'm baking brownies for you. I've got to make sure they're not burning." With that, she pushes through the swinging door to the kitchen.

As she goes in, Gus pads out into the dining room. Hearing my voice, he turns his head and trots toward me. When I don't rise out of the chair to meet him, he slows his approach, his demeanor suddenly guarded. Gus circles the wheelchair, taking great huffing sniffs, and places himself in the chair's path.

He makes it clear that he dislikes and distrusts the contraption. He fixes me with his droopy eyes, and does a hound dog's low whine, punctuated by quiet, plaintive woofs. *Stand up, stand up.* I make fun of people who lie to their pets. "I'm going to the store; I'll be right back . . ." (even though you know you'll be gone for hours). "We're not going to the vet . . ." (that's exactly where you're going). We all do it; I try not to. But when I reach out to Gus from the chair and tell him, "I'm okay," we both know I'm lying.

The center hallway in our apartment ends in a "T"; the master bedroom to the right, and to the left, a small spare bedroom that, over the years, has become my realm, my den. Now repurposed for convalescence, it is barely recognizable; a hospital room, but with carpets and my own books on the shelves. My bathroom is reconfigured with strategically placed grip bars.

Within the glass-and-marble shower enclosure are more grip bars, and gleaming under the overhead light, a chrome and plastic chair—a sadly appropriate throne for a damaged king, returning from battle.

———

Same war, different front. The rehab program at Mount Sinai Hospital has earned a reputation similar to that of Johns Hopkins. It's a smaller facility, and not quite as elaborately equipped, but as I'm about to learn, something as basic as an oversized rubber band or a stack of red solo cups can be dynamic tools in the hands of a skilled therapist. And I soon meet that therapist. Will, a tall, slender man in his thirties, greets me on the third floor. He has a friendly face, impeccable posture, and what has to be a theatrically trained voice.

Will approaches my wheelchair; I stand to shake his hand, but it's difficult and I begin to pitch forward. In extending his hand and grasping mine, he steadies me into a full standing position.

"I'm Mike," I say. "Sorry, I'm a little wobbly. My internal gyroscope is out of whack."

"Your proprioception is way off. Let's see what we can do about that."

The word "proprioception" derives from the Latin "*proprius*," meaning "individual or one's own," and "*capere*," meaning "to take or grasp." It is the sense of the relative position of one's own body parts, and the strength of effort being employed in any movement. Some people refer to it as their "sixth sense"; others would say, "It's where I am in space." I can barely pronounce it, but I can apply the word to my experience. From our first meeting, Dr. Theodore had explained that I should expect problems with my proprioception after surgery, specifically altering my equilibrium and stability. He framed it this way: "If your proprioception is impaired, you have the sensation, for example, that you can't stand in a dark room without falling over." I hadn't anticipated that it would be this confusing and disorienting.

Will continues his evaluation. "And of course you have Parkinson's, too," he says. "Which already impairs your ability to walk, at baseline."

I affect a shocked expression. "I have Parkinson's?"

Most days I travel to and from treatment at Mount Sinai by wheel-chair. I hold my walker on my lap while Belinda, my current health aide and pilot, swerves in and out of pedestrian traffic on the Upper East Side. There is a certain entitlement that comes with the job of being the wheelchair pusher. Belinda takes up as much space and goes as fast or slow as Belinda wants, no matter how many people are blocking her path. She uses me as a blunt instrument to hack her way through the crowd. I can't help but think that some little old lady is going to be run over, and the last face she'll see will be mine. Sam, Tracy, and Nina often walk with us. We are a tiny parade; same time, same route, same show, winding its way to the hospital. If only we had giant balloons and a float.

I don't like sitting in a wheelchair, but as a practical matter, given Man-hattan's grid of one-way streets, the distance traveled from my apartment to the out-patient rehab facility, a few blocks away, is more easily accom-plished this way than by vehicle. Even so, there is a vulnerability and ex-posure that comes with being seen in a wheelchair in public. This is a new experience for me; one I would rather have skipped. In truth, I think more attention is paid to the chair than to the person riding in it, even by those who begrudgingly make way for it. The exception is when they are in danger of being run over by a wheelchair—which is often the case, given Belinda's bulldozer technique.

Asses and Elbows

We refer to people in wheelchairs as wheelchair-bound. What does that mean, exactly? Wheelchair-bound suggests that one is bound to the chair; held hostage. It contains you. Perhaps the person who is used to mobility (and the unrestricted use of their body parts) looks at the chair as a conces-sion, as an instrument of surrender. Whereas, to one who is disabled to a point where independent movement is not an option, the chair is a means of freedom to move.

I relate to the concept that this way of moving around is a reality of my future, as in "I'm bound for a wheelchair." At some point, using a wheelchair is a likelihood; it's only a question of when.

In the past year or two, I have used one sparingly, under certain circumstances to save time and energy. I am relieved to have access to it whenever I need to cross a vast amount of space in a short amount of time. On trips overseas, for example, airport transfers make a wheelchair essential.

Unless I know the person who is pushing me in the wheelchair, it can be a frustrating and isolating experience, allowing someone else to determine the direction I'm going and rate of speed I can travel. The pusher is in charge. From the point-of-view of the occupant of the chair, it's a world of asses and elbows. There's something, too, about a wheelchair that has an effect on my voice. No one can hear me. To compensate, I raise my voice and suddenly feel like Joan Crawford in *What Ever Happened to Baby Jane?*, barking out orders. But no one is listening. For someone who is used to having mobility and a sense of free will, being in the wheelchair is completely the opposite. I am at the mercy of the person steering me. They will put me into a corner, or up against the wall, and I will have no say in it. I can hear something I want to respond to, but I can't turn around and see it.

Generally, the person in control is a stranger, an airport or hotel employee. I'm sure that if we could ever look each other in the eye, we'd recognize our mutual humanity. But often in the wheelchair, I'm luggage. I'm not expected to say much. Just sit still. Delivery to my destination is just another task to be finished in their busy day.

On a recent trip, going through airport security in a wheelchair was excruciating. If I stayed in the chair, I couldn't go through the scanner. I had to pull off to the side and be subjected to a thorough pat down, then wait while the wheelchair was meticulously swabbed and examined. My attendant was surprised when I suggested it would be much easier if I just walked through the scanner. He couldn't seem to comprehend that the wheelchair was provisional. I don't consider it necessary, an important distinction that is often lost on those who steer.

"I can walk, I just can't walk far. That's why I use the chair." He wasn't hearing it. I don't walk quickly or efficiently, but I have my cane, and I can make the decision when to use the chair. You can't explain that to everybody. When you stand and actually start to take steps, it's as if no one around you wants to believe it ("He can walk!"). Once they have seen the wheelchair, they believe you're immobile.

I used my cane to approach the scanner, and then handed that off to a TSA employee before I went through, picked it up on the other side, and used it for support until the chair came through.

It was clear that rising from the chair and demonstrating the ability to operate independently rattled my handler. "Here, get in the chair," he insisted.

"I'm all right. I just want to stretch my legs for a minute."

This left him befuddled. "But here's the chair," he repeated.

I would've liked to be vertical for a few more minutes, but I felt obliged to climb back in the chair of silence and be delivered to the gate. No one listens to luggage.

You Don't Know What You've Got 'Til It's Gone

I have to learn to walk again; to reclaim my mobility, remaster my motion. I consider this fundamental to my therapy—for me, it all starts and ends with walking. And I understand that it's more complicated than that. So many tiny disciplines have to be observed, and neglected muscles and ligaments need to be restored. I'm exhausted by the effort I've already put in at Johns Hopkins, and daunted by how much work I still have to do. It's like being nibbled to death by ducks.

Back in the days of carefree ambling, I would have considered the topic of walking to be rather pedestrian. Now the acts of stepping, strolling, hiking, and perambulating have become an obsession. I watch Esmé gliding through the kitchen, grabbing an apple while opening the fridge door for a coconut water, closing it with a quick shift of her hip and pirouetting out the swinging door at the other end of the room. Down in the lobby, my neighbor and her daughter are quickstepping to catch a taxi. I spy on a man walking with a slight limp, which he counterbalances with a bag of groceries. I secretly watch the way they all move. Easy, breezy, catlike, or with a limp, every one of them is far better at it than me.

It may be that the most difficult, miraculous thing we do, physically, is to walk. It's one of the first things on the agenda, and we do it before we realize how impossible the whole exercise is. Tracy and I have four children; we know the drill. My mind can pull up images of Sam, for example, at age one. With a pat on the butt, I sent him trucking across the living room rug. I counted each tiny footfall. After some confident toddling, Sam reached the edge of our ottoman coffee table. His knees buckled momentarily. He took a breath, steadied himself, his oversized head wobbling, and broke away from his support. Suddenly standing alone, with nothing around him but a sea of carpet, he saw Tracy waiting for him. He quickened his step, stumbled, and fell into her arms.

Now, on occasion, her husband does the same thing.

It's uncanny how this memory loop of Sam's first steps mirrors my situation, post-surgery. I've read that while learning how to walk, toddlers fall an average of twenty-one times an hour. In my sessions at Mount Sinai, I swear there are days when—if my physical therapist didn't catch me by my arm or shoulder or the scruff of my neck—I'd beat that average.

That kind of physical rescue from an imminent fall is often mirrored by an emotional rescue, in the form of support from my family. Tracy comes to every therapy session during the first week, and then continues to drop in and observe my progress in the weeks that follow, always with smiles, hugs, and words of encouragement. Sam doesn't miss many sessions, either. He is wholly focused on each exercise, each repetition, each little victory over a particular challenge, and each temporary defeat. He never looks out the window; he never checks his cell phone. When I complain that something is difficult for me to do, he is always there with, "That's because you're old, Dad." Believe it or not, that makes me feel better.

———

We all naturally adjust to obstacles, and visual and physical stimuli, in our own way. Since I can't anticipate or elude obstructions, I have to implement a regimen of self-observation and correction. I can't be sure, without a visual check, which foot I'm leading with, left or right. I'm off-balance if my head is too far forward or tilting too far back. I have to consider the mechanics of each movement.

It's tough. With PD and the aftermath of the surgery, something as simple as remaining upright is often sabotaged by a rogue army of misfiring neurons. I try to stay organized. I have memorized a litany of admonitions, not unlike my golfer's list of swing thoughts: Keep my head centered over my hips; hips over my knees; no hyperextending; stay in line with my feet; eyes forward; shoulders back; chest out; lead with the pelvis. All of this kinetic vigilance can dissolve in a nanosecond of panic, or come apart with some other distraction. A tiny nervous jolt or spasm, and like a house of cards in a sudden gust of wind, the only messages that make it through the debris are: *Don't fall. Don't fall. Don't fall . . .*

Get up.

Will to Walk

When I first met my PT, Will, I immediately knew two things about the guy: One, he was determined to get me walking again safely; and two, he had been, at some point, an actor or performer (*that voice!*). I ask him, out of the blue, if he still works on Broadway. I'm not surprised when he answers, "Nope, I gave it up. This pays better." Now I know he's smart, too.

Will is focused on helping me develop my own system of kinetic priorities. The key to walking to the other side of the room is not *being* there, but *getting* there. I rise from chairs and lean forward to the point where I'm convinced I'll topple over onto my face and break my nose. I pick up a beanbag from one end of a table, walk around a series of traffic cones to reach the other end, and put the beanbag in a cup. Then I side-step around the table to the stack of beanbags, and do it all again. I'm over any curiosity as to why these specific exercises are beneficial—I figure they're too weird not to have a purpose. But Will explains it anyway. For him, PT is a serious endeavor, taken on with honorable aspirations. I feel a responsibility to him to succeed, just as I felt a responsibility to Dr. Theodore to not fall, injure my back, and damage his work.

From the outset, Will gives my Parkinson's and spinal surgery equal weight, never dealing with the impact of one without acknowledging the complicating factor of the other. He's not a specialist; he can deal with whatever a patient presents, including my combination of problems. Will knows how to separate one condition from the other. Parkinson's dictates the speed and trajectory of my movement; while the stress on my spinal cord creates a lack of sensation and affects my proprioception. We work on the mechanics and kinetics of walking, with attention paid to both of these issues. It's a complex algorithm, and there are no easy shortcuts.

Over the next two months, we do everything from the basics—stretching, core work, getting in and out of chairs—to obstacle courses and ball tosses (without toppling), all in pursuit of the holy grail: walking independently. I walk for miles in one little stretch of hallway on the third floor at Mount Sinai, using a variety of different implements: a walker, two canes, then one cane. The truth is, I never master the cane. I have trouble negotiating my own two legs, and now I have a third. How do I make this work? I'm captain of my own ship; I don't need an extra oar.

I travel back and forth, always with some form of support. Hospital floors are hard surfaces, and even at 5' 5", it's a long way down. In the doorways at each end of the hall, I experience tremendous stutter-stepping. Something about my PD hates crossing thresholds; it interrupts my progress and forces me to make a choice to continue. If I encounter someone while passing through a doorway, unable to avoid them, I freeze. Only when they move am I released.

Twist and Shout

There are other aspects to my spring and summer therapy at Mount Sinai, such as the occupational piece of it: more carrying, lifting, bathroom safety, bed-making, and sock-tugging. I take this seriously, too, and I now manage to put my own socks on without mechanical intervention.

Specifically related to my Parkinson's, I also participate in five weeks of speech therapy. It's common for Parkinson's patients, particularly during later stages of their disease, to slur and mumble their words, or to experience problems speaking clearly and loudly enough for others to hear. I didn't think I would enjoy this additional therapy, but I do. Speaking loudly and clearly is more difficult than one would think. It's something new and different in rehab, and at least if I screw up, I don't fall down.

My instructor, Siobhan, provides me a list of words in different sequences, and reads me snippets of prose, parts of which she quizzes me on after reading. I answer the questions or reorder the words, whatever is required. There's a bizarre element included in all of this: I'm in a small room, two doors down from where a half-dozen patients are working intently with their therapists, and I'm screaming at the top of my lungs. That's the secret of this therapy—it has to be at maximum volume in order to improve weakened vocal cords. Siobhan often gives me homework, and I complete the assignment by calling her answering service and shouting my results.

Each day's work ends with her handing me a piece of journalism or some other literary material, which she asks me to belt out for all of Mount Sinai Hospital to enjoy. I receive today's piece of paper, and without delay, I rip into it. After two sentences, I realize I am sharing the exquisitely crafted words of my esteemed brother-in-law, Michael Pollan. The piece relates to his work on hallucinogens. That night, I pass on this information to Michael P., adding that "I may have convinced someone with a broken hip to try psilocybin therapy." He is decidedly pleased.

13

A CROWDED HOUSE

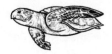

REM sleep brings strange nightmares and a few sweet dreams. In some, I can't move; I am paralyzed. In others, I'm as able-bodied as I was as a kid. This nocturnal brain activity seems normal, but what happens tonight is definitely abnormal. It's a waking dream; my eyes are open. *I can't be seeing what I'm seeing.* It's a hallucination, a delusion; an unwelcome flashback to my post-op mind warp. If I close my eyes and still see it, then I will know it's a nightmare. My eyes shut—and he's gone. Eyes open—he's there again, bigger and badder than ever: a hooded figure, his bearded face awash in green luminescence, looming at the foot of my bed. From my angle, he's a wizard, or Obi-Wan Kenobi, or maybe Satan, glowing in the dark.

Then, I get it . . . it's not the Dark Lord, after all; it is just Frank. Frank's presence represents everything that is fucked-up about my circumstance. Until you've experienced it, it's difficult to appreciate the creepiness of being observed while you sleep.

Frank, a nice enough guy, is my nighttime aide. An avid biker, he parks his Harley in front of our building. He arrives at 8 p.m. and takes over from the day shift. This means that I am never alone, and it is suffocating. Frank watches the hockey game with me, or puts up with my current binge, *Peaky Blinders*. At some point after I fall asleep, he ensconces himself in the recliner across from my bed in the den, pulls up the hood of his sweatshirt to shade his bearded jowls, and jams in his earbuds. His iPhone bathes his face in an eerie glow as he texts his wife. Every once in a while, he peers up to assure himself that I haven't spontaneously combusted.

In the dead of night, I stir awake and shudder. Emerging from half-sleep, I am dazed and confused by the presence of this hooded, cross-legged Beelzebub. He accepts my stare, and asks, "Hey, man. Do you need to go pee?"

And so it goes. At 8 a.m., the daytime home health aides arrive. After brushing my teeth and combing my hair, they help me dress, and we're on our way to the rehab facility. These aides are associates in a sort of enterprise—the business of restoring my health. They observe each day's therapy session and encourage my efforts.

With today's rehab over, my aide Belinda wheels me down Madison Avenue's crowded sidewalk at her regular Indy 500 pace. "You looked good in there today," she huffs. "But take your time, don't rush."

The wheelchair bounces over a curb (*or was that someone's foot?*). "Thanks. Right back at you, Belinda."

With dinner finished, the night shift takes over and stays with me until the morning. I have the most grief with the nighttime aides. I'm sure they'd say the same about me. None of us are at fault; it's just that the whole premise is flawed. While the day shift seems invested in my recovery, the night shift attends to me as if I'm of an advanced age: infirm and disabled, a fragile hospice patient with limited prospects. Actually, that's not entirely fair. They are dedicated and capable health professionals who are concerned for my welfare. But the impression I get is that they just don't want me to fall on their watch.

What is remarkable to me about this time period—from the ICU, to rehab at Johns Hopkins, and the return to New York for more physical therapy—is how microscopic my world has become. I'm a single-cell organism in a petri dish, under observation twenty-four hours a day. But this situation is far too intimate for my present disposition. I'm finally in my own home again, and my supreme goal—to get back on my feet and begin operating independently—runs counter to the objectives of the nocturnal occupying force, who want to limit my movement in this, my personal space. By design, the night aides' priority must be to avoid the slightest risk.

Prevention, not progress.

Parkinson's has robbed me of the luxury of spontaneity. I can't initiate any new activity without a careful assessment of my physical circumstance and mental alertness. Being observed so intensely, though, is a new kind of constriction. The surgery has rendered me unbearably dependent. I bristle at steadying hands that reach out to support me—by my judgment, most times, unnecessarily. As I make my way to the bathroom, I'm watched over like a baby in a bathtub. My muttered objections soon escalate to audible complaints. I negotiate to be allowed a least a few cautious steps on my own, but as with the nurses at Johns Hopkins, my home aides' mandate is clear: No walking without assistance.

Walks in the Park

My days in physical therapy at Mount Sinai are a wholly different experience. Progress is made and measured, and I grow more confident that soon I'll be able to walk safely. I really want this, and with pride in the quality of my effort, I will go through any amount of pain or pressure to achieve my goal.

With Will, my PT, the work is steady and intense. Out of frustration, I balk at certain exercises, but he insists that I persist. The inspiration I draw from the other patients in the facility is a big factor in my ability to push through. Many are in far more dire circumstances than me; strokes, severe car accidents, spinal damage, loss of limbs. When needed, this is a shot of reality.

All the while, my family, Nina, and that day's aide, Belinda or Marcus (a pleasant gentleman—and a much more careful wheelchair-pusher) are there to mark my progress and celebrate it with me.

Eventually, after months of focused effort, I am free of it all. No walker, no cane. I'm able to manage the nighttime hours alone now, without an aide. When I close the bathroom door, I'm the only one inside of it. The daytime aides are still here, and they're helpful; they acknowledge my progress and encourage me toward independence.

When I finish the prescribed therapy at Mount Sinai, I know I'll need to continue daily workouts at home. Will sends me off with good advice.

"Don't be in a hurry to get this done," he counsels. "You have to be okay with taking a step back. This is a long process. You made an investment of blood, sweat, and tears in this therapy, and spilled plenty of all three. But you have to keep at it. I'm sorry to tell you that the work never stops."

It's not easy to hear. But I resolve to kick ass, even if it is my own.

They Say It's Your Birthday

Days after rehab ends, I celebrate my birthday. Tracy has gathered a dinner party in our apartment with five other couples. For many of these friends, I've been missing in action for the past six months, and they have questions about my experiences. I run through it for anyone who asks, and to my relief, their comments lean more toward "You look good," than "Looks like you had a rough time." So that's reassuring.

After dinner, Tracy taps on her wineglass and rises to speak. I'm surprised, because she doesn't often give toasts. Our eyes meet across the table. With a slight smile, I raise an eyebrow. *A toast, really? Wow.*

She begins, "I know we're all here to wish Mike a happy birthday. But I want to say something else, too." She fixes her gaze on me and pauses. "Mike, this has been such a tough year for you. What you've been through is incredible. The surgery, rehab at Johns Hopkins, and at Mount Sinai."

And then, to our friends around the table: "He has worked so hard. Every day, day after day. He had to learn to walk all over again. He is amazing." Her eyes come back to me and she smiles. "Not that he still isn't a pain in the ass, sometimes."

This makes me laugh. "Guilty," I interject.

She raises her glass. "I'm so proud of you, Michael. We all are. The kids, everybody. We love you. *I love you*, and I believe in you. Happy birthday. May the next year be a little easier. For all of us."

Everyone raises their glass, and I tip mine toward Tracy. I hope through all the clinking and birthday wishes, she hears me. "I love you, too."

Three years prior, on my fifty-fourth birthday, Tracy surprised me with an incredible gift. Presenting it to me required us to make a stop en route to my celebratory dinner. Although our reservation was at a restaurant down in Greenwich Village, Tracy asked the car to turn uptown, and it let us out at the 105th Street entrance to Central Park. She took my hand as we crossed through the gates of the Conservatory Garden, one of my favorite spots in the city. Many long walks with Gus have included a stop at one of the benches here, which overlook the gardens. Gus likes to clamber onto the wooden slats and muscle me over to take up more than his share of the seat.

On that warm summer birthday night, the park was as beautiful as ever, the air heavy with the perfume of wisteria. Tracy led me toward the western border of the garden. "It's not a pony, is it?" I asked. "You know, we don't have room for a pony."

"That's just the fertilizer smell. Anyway, you've already got a pony. His name is Gus."

She stopped when we reached a particular bench, and called my attention to a small plaque, a dedication plate. Tracy had made a donation to the Central Park Conservancy, for which she was allowed to dedicate a park bench. This one was mine. The inscription read "For Mike Fox and Gus. True New Yorkers."

My first thought was: *How amazing. A perfect gift.* My second thought: *I don't know how much longer I will be able to walk this far with Gus.*

Years ago, before the tumor on my spine had even announced itself, my legs were weakening, my endurance diminishing. Parkinson's is a thief, and now it was taking away something as simple but precious as the ability to walk my dog in the park.

By unknowingly placing such a wonderful prize just beyond my grasp, the greatest gift Tracy had given me that night, was incentive.

Flash forward. It's the day after Tracy's dinner party for my fifty-seventh birthday. Today, I'm back in the Conservatory Garden, the perfect location for a rehab graduation victory lap, or more like a victory straightaway. I'm going to attempt my first short walk on my own—away from any facility, without a cane, walker, or the assistance of an aide. Schuyler is with me, along with her boyfriend, Will Savage, an Ivy League baseball phenom who's just been drafted by the Detroit Tigers. They push me up Fifth Avenue in my rental wheelchair (hopefully soon to be returned), to the entrance of the garden.

Very near my bench, I rise from the chair, place my feet an appropriate distance apart, shift my weight from side to side like I'm about to swing a nine-iron, pick up my right foot, and press forward. Heel first, then transfer weight, and the left foot follows. Now I'm showboating. I make it about one hundred feet or so when, detecting a wobble in my step, Will hustles to catch up with me. Instead of grabbing my arm, he offers his own, and after a semi-stumble, I gratefully take it. He instinctively understands that the situation does not call for him to rescue me, but for me to reach out to him. It's a subtle distinction, but a big difference. I rest my hand on Will's arm for a second or two, then let go and carry on.

Schuyler captures the moment on her iPhone. We send a video to Dr. Theodore, with whom I stay in regular contact. He'll love it; he can put it on his reel.

I knew that recovery would be a slog, but I didn't fully anticipate how aware I would be of my state of mind, my emotions. Optimism has always been the norm for me. But perhaps with age, or through the rigors of this experience, I now find it easier to drift into melancholy; to lose my enthusiasm for the task at hand. On this day, I'm relieved that my walk in the park with Schuyler and Will provides an antidote. In fact, as much as I can immerse myself in their stories, their victories, and their lives, my own becomes much less important. It's a welcome shift.

Everyone—family and friends—has been really supportive. They remind me that I have a life to step back into, which encourages me to be forward-thinking.

14

BREAKING DAD

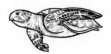

During my recent months of rehab, in between morning and afternoon therapy sessions at Mount Sinai, my golf buddies Harlan Coben and George Stephanopoulos regularly dropped by my apartment to have lunch with me. My golf buddies are encouraging. They buoy me with their friendship and company, and remind me that the quicker I heal, the sooner I return to the links.

Today will be the last time we get together like this, because rehab has ended, summer is arriving, and busy family schedules will disrupt our routine.

Harlan calls ahead with his usual order. "Chicken noodle soup," he requests.

"Yeah, I can set that up," I promise. "See you at one."

At a towering (to me) 6' 5", with a clean-shaven dome, Harlan would be intimidating if he wasn't so affable. We blather about golf and politics; anything but my spine. It may have to do with the fact that he is one of the world's best-selling novelists, but he tells a good story over a bowl of soup, usually related to his far-ranging business travels. Netflix adapted a few of his books into wildly popular miniseries, and he's been zipping back and forth between production locations in Europe. Harlan is especially beloved by the French. *Pourquoi?*

He shrugs. "What can I say? I'm the Jerry Lewis of mystery writers."

George stops by at the end of his workday at *Good Morning America*. Still trim and fit, with more hair than a Portuguese water dog, he was first introduced to me back in the '90s, in preparation for my role as a young political operative in *The American President*. The similarities went beyond our shared lack of height. I had a lot of hair then, too.

You never know with George—he could've just had pancakes with Trump, or shared a cab with Andrew Cuomo. Harlan and I goad him into divulging his political insights and opinions, and he never disappoints. Whatever Harlan and I have for lunch, George has the healthier version. But he is always a sucker for a popsicle—usually lemon-lime, my go-to palate cleanser.

Before I head downstairs for my afternoon workout, and George departs for home to take a nap, and Harlan goes back to his place to bang out another novel, we talk golf. A big PGA tournament is coming up at Harlan's club, and he invites the two of us to walk the course with the pros. I realize that I can't possibly walk the course anytime soon, so we don't discuss it much further.

A few weeks later, Harlan, George, and I will watch the tournament together; not at the club, but on the TV in my living room. Harlan brings over official PGA programs. We're in awe at these pros, who are absolutely shredding the course that has humbled and exposed us so many times. Golf only makes good television if you're a golfer. But for those that love the game, it stokes a fire to play again. You just can't wait to get out there and swing a club.

As events transpire, my return to the game will not happen as soon as I hoped. Unexpectedly, I'll soon find myself in a bunker, with no way to dig out. Life, already in flux, is about to change again. What remains constant is my friendship with these two guys. They will be there for me, round for round, no matter how deep the rough.

My Aides Decamp

Eventually, I regain my independence, free to move in a world beyond the distance between one end of an antiseptic hospital corridor and the other. At last, I am able to stroll around the apartment without assistance. My gait is better. I have progressed from walker to cane to elbow-holding aide, to hands-free truckin' down the hallway.

Now I am able to say goodbye to my daytime aides. I've grown fond of Belinda, the Richard Petty of home health care. On her final day with me at home, I offer my appreciation and tell her I hope to see her again, but miles away from a wheelchair.

Marcus, the rehab cheerleader, is pressed into duty one more weekend, to travel with us to Aquinnah's graduation. Aquinnah took a gap year before attending university. Schuyler graduated last spring from a liberal arts college in California.

It's a sprawling campus, so I need Marcus to steer me in a wheelchair. I trust him to make sure I don't miss a beat. As expected on an early summer day in North Carolina, the heat is oppressive, and with no breeze, it's constant and inescapable. But Marcus is steady and uncomplaining. When I introduce him to Aquinnah, I am happy that she takes time out to thank him. My beautiful daughter beams with accomplishment. I'm so proud of her that I don't give a shit about who sees me in a wheelchair. Aquinnah is just relieved that I'm able to attend the graduation, so soon after surgery.

"Dood, I'm so happy that you're here. You look good."

"Yeah, I used to be on TV."

She laughs, and expresses regret that she couldn't make it up to Baltimore

to visit me at Johns Hopkins. I tell her that I understood—the final se-
mester before graduation was hectic, and I wanted her to concentrate on
reaching this day.

So much of what's important in life seems to sneak up on me. So
much time and energy invested in getting ready to go someplace, and
then getting there, that the sensation of being there is a revelation. Look
where I am. Look what happened. It's a blur, like living several lives at
once. As Aquinnah accepts her diploma, I consider not just my journey
to this milestone, but hers—the unique and demanding path she created
for herself.

Charming, affable, and lovely, with what I call her *resting-on-the-beach
face*, Aquinnah is smarter than two of me, and tougher than I'll ever be.
Her work ethic is staggering. A ballet dancer since she was four, classically
trained at the School of American Ballet and later Ballet Academy East,
Aquinnah had reached a professional level. I cringe at the thought that I may
have been so occupied with my travails and injuries, that I never fully recognized the sacrifice, physical and emotional and temporal, that Aquinnah
has made over the years.

There were many missed holiday vacations, when she and Schuyler
danced in *George Balanchine's The Nutcracker* with New York City Ballet.
Sky dropped out of dance at the end of fifth grade, but Aquinnah persisted,
in a big way. She felt that if she took even a few days off, she would lose her
flexibility and be out of shape.

By the time she was fifteen, the School of American Ballet required an
even greater effort, essentially full-time. To continue, Aquinnah would
have to be home-schooled or transfer her academic education to the Professional Children's School. She chose to remain at her current high school,
and instead changed ballet schools. Still, she wanted to make dance her
career. She maintained a six-day-a-week schedule, attending classes during
the day and the Ballet Academy East at night. She applied to the college of
her dreams and was accepted, but she knew she had to be all-in for ballet,

or all-in for college. She decided to defer college for a year and went to Miami as a student apprentice with the Miami City Ballet, and at the end of that commitment, she was offered a job with the Washington Ballet's Studio Company in D.C. It was clear that she had succeeded in her goal of becoming a professional ballet dancer. The offer was there. She weighed carefully the choice between ballet and university. In the end, she decided that she would dance at college.

By the time Aquinnah was a freshman in high school, we were aware of the toll that ballet was taking on her body. Calves and hip flexors were stressed to the point of agony, and she dislocated her shoulder a couple of times, broke her foot, and fractured the tibial plateau in her knee. While the knee was still slowly recovering, she had surgery to repair her shoulder. It was painful. She was seeing a chiropractor regularly, and an acupuncturist weekly. This treatment was essential. Also, dancers' toes take a savage beating. She'd wear out a new pair of pointe shoes every few days. One particular brand of shoe caused her to lose both of her big toenails. She left them on Schuyler's pillow, which wasn't appreciated.

After the graduation ceremony, Marcus guides my chair to a shady patch of lawn next to the chapel, within which Aquinnah has just received her diploma. Tracy, Sam, Sky, and Esmé are there, ready to take some pictures. Tracy says, "Aquinnah, let's get a shot with you and your dad."

Aquinnah puts her hand on my arm and bends down for the photo. I smile. "If it's okay, I'll stand for this one." And I do. And she hugs me.

Independence Day

July arrives, and my family and I resume our normal summer schedule. We use our home on Long Island as a midsummer base. I continue therapy on my own, and my walking improves, slowly and steadily, although I've granted myself the assistance of an industrial four-prong mega-cane. The prongs may not be the best idea, because they encourage me to cheat and use the cane as a crutch, as opposed to a metronomic device to measure stride. But I get along, and can keep up with the group.

Oh, but there is one incident. After enjoying dinner at a hip restaurant in Sag Harbor, I pay the check and we make our way toward our waiting car. We have to pass through the crowded bar, with several archways and loose carpets. All of this visual busyness triggers one of those mini-moments of panic that cause overstriding, which degrades into festination. Alarmed by the threshold of an arch, my shuffling feet trip up on a carpet edge and I tip forward, extending my hands to cushion my fall. Unfortunately, one hand is still holding the cane, and my thumb gets trapped and bent awkwardly, tearing a ligament. I rise, embarrassed, tempted to offer a sheepish bow to the now-staring diners in the establishment. (*Is that Michael J. Fox?*) I check out my thumb—yep, it's officially damaged. Later I make plans with a hand surgeon to have the tendon reattached.

In early August, my family and I board a ferry for two weeks on Martha's Vineyard, blissfully unaware that the thumb incident presages something worse. On the positive side, I am discouraged from overusing the cane, and as a result, my stride is much improved.

———

I love this island. After more than twenty summers vacationing here, I know it like home ground. Tracy and her family have been coming to the Vineyard since she was born. They established their summer idyll in the town of Aquinnah, which not coincidentally, is also the name of our recently graduated daughter.

Every day, we make our way to the beach, an unspoiled strand of gorgeous New England shoreline, protected by towering dunes. Long before I had any problem with my spine, these dunes challenged me. I'd have to climb up one side of the monstrous wave of sand on all fours, and slide down the other side on my butt toward the ocean.

We have a silly game we play at the start of every summer season, kind of a family tradition: The first person to the crest of the dune throws their arms in the air and shouts, "I'm the king of the mountain!" On my post-surgery return, I decide that I'm taking this year's honors. I'm under doctor's orders not to carry anything, so I take the opportunity to hobble past my beach umbrella-chair-blanket-and-towel-toting wife and children. Even with this advantage, I still have to negotiate the last part of the ascent on all fours. I'm feeling great—until I reach the sandy summit. Once there, I sputter out the obligatory declaration of royalty, only to find I can't throw my arms in the air without tweaking my spine, losing my balance, and tipping over. That takes the swagger out of the whole thing, and I ignominiously slither down the seaside slope of the dune. Even so, I am the first one on the beach. *It's good to be king.*

I look at the sunlight flickering off the shore-break, and see a man tossing a soggy tennis ball to an enthusiastic border collie. I miss Gus. It feels odd that he's not with us; after all, this is his turf; this is where we found each other. But his aversion to the water has never changed. He really hates it. And he's especially distrustful of the ocean. He's not crazy about hot sand, either, and he can never find enough shade. So, to avoid stressing him out, he's at doggy camp in Connecticut, while we enjoy the sun and waves in Massachusetts.

Martha's Vineyard is a dichotomy. It is verdant, with country roads that ramble under exquisite leafy arbors, and roll past grassy meadows dotted with sheep. The caveat is, we're not the only ones who love it. Over the summer, the Vineyard receives hordes of tourists on bicycles, mopeds, in cars and trucks, clogging the streets of Edgartown and Vineyard Haven with Boston-style traffic jams. But save for a shortlist of locals—many of whose surnames can be found on the *Mayflower*'s manifest—we're all tourists on the Vineyard, so we don't complain.

I'm thriving here. Leaving the island is the last thing on my mind, until a script arrives from my agent, with an interesting offer. Spike Lee is producing a film by a young protégé, Stefon Bristol. *See You Yesterday* is a time-travel movie, a nod to *Back to the Future*, with a compelling twist. A teenage girl, reeling from the death of her older brother at the hands of the police, manufactures the means for time travel in order to reverse history and save him. The filmmakers want me for a cameo, in the role of the girl's science teacher, who is dubious about time travel. It's a small part, a bit of a wink, but I like it. This is a low-stress way to ease back into work.

My scenes are set to shoot on the Monday of our last week on Martha's Vineyard. It's a one-day commitment, with travel days on either side; I'll easily make it back in time to close out the vacation with Tracy, Esmé, and Aquinnah. Schuyler has work to do in the city, so we'll travel to New York together on Sunday.

Legend of the Fall

Parents with multiple children are often asked if they have a favorite. I always say, "Yeah, whichever one I'm with." Tonight, I'm with Schuyler, and I couldn't be happier. We sit at the kitchen table, eating take-out Italian and discussing Sky's fledgling career. She works for a clinic that provides support for adolescents with anxiety disorders. Sensitive and empathetic, Sky cares a lot about the kids she works with. Some people *see* the world around them; Schuyler *feels* it. She makes me want to sing the theme song from *The Mary Tyler Moore Show*.

Curious about how to progress in her field, or perhaps in another, we discuss her options and opportunities at length. She has a secondary interest in working in communications and children's television, and she's also considering getting her master's in health and public policy.

It's a good talk. I wrap it up by reminding her, "Well, Sky, you don't have to figure out the rest of your life tonight."

She laughs and tosses her napkin on her plate. "Well then, when will I figure it out?"

"That, I don't know," I answer. "I guess there's no time like the future." We clear our dishes. "Hey, Sky, do me a favor?"

"Sure."

I reach up to the shelf behind the kitchen table and retrieve my folded script pages. "Do you mind running tomorrow's lines with me?"

She smiles and says, "I'd love to."

I used to be able to take an entire script for *Family Ties*, look at it for five minutes, and know every word. Not so much anymore. Maybe it's PD, or maybe it's just being fifty-seven. Who knows?

I'm fairly solid on these lines, but practice never hurts. And it's fun.

My daughter reads the other characters' lines, and without being too weird about it, almost performs them. "Hey, wait a minute," I say. "What about acting? Didn't you take a couple of classes last year?"

This cracks her up. "Yeah. But, god, no. Absolutely not. That was for fun, not for profit. I couldn't take the pressure."

"Yeah, it gives you Parkinson's."

We go through the scenes a few more times. It's getting late, so I let her off the hook. "Honey, I'm up at six fifteen. I've got to get some sleep."

She pauses. "I don't think I should leave. I should stay and be here for you in the morning, to fix you breakfast."

"You should go back to your apartment. You have to be at work early, yourself." I offer a slight smile. "Look, I know you and Mom talked about this, and decided I shouldn't be alone. But I need to do this by myself."

Sky packs up the leftovers and stores them in the fridge. "It's not like it's some kind of conspiracy to spy on you, or babysit you, or keep you from living your life. We just care about you. We love you."

"I love you, too, and I love that you care about me. But you can care about me without having to *take* care of me."

After Sky collects her bag, we walk to the door. With lingering hesitation, she asks, "Are you sure?"

In a gentle tone, I respond, "Stop. You have to go. It's late, so don't take the subway. Take an Uber. I'll be fine. I'll call you on the way back from the set tomorrow." We hug as the elevator arrives. She steps in. I listen to it rumble down to the lobby, and look around at the empty apartment. I am alone.

———

This is what happens.

The next morning, I set out for the kitchen to grab breakfast; not much, maybe a piece of toast and a swallow of juice. There will be no coffee; Tracy's coffee maker was engineered by Mercedes-Benz, and I never read the manual. I am wearing sweatpants and the Tom Petty T-shirt I slept in. In less than two hours, I won't have that shirt anymore—an EMT with a pair of shears will cut it off on my way to the emergency room.

But in the moment, I am pleased. "Right chuffed," as the English would say, to be going to work. I am in excellent form, my walking smooth. Emboldened, I pick up the pace a bit, just because I can, realizing there is no one here to chide me. I kick it up another notch and turn the corner into the kitchen, a sharp right. I steady myself by lightly touching the doorframe, not for support, but for balance. Then I plow ahead. Three steps into the breakfast nook, I execute a quick left to avoid the banquette—and that's where it all goes sideways. Something distracts me. I lose control, one foot crossing over the other foot. I stop too suddenly, slide on the tile, and down I go.

Get up.

Nope. I can't get up. I delay that impulse, and instead survey my cranium for any cracks or contusions; my face for any broken bones or teeth.

No blood. At least I avoided serious head-to-floor contact. My brain seems okay; no headache, and I don't feel nauseous. I am, however, a little confused. I can't understand how I could have done this to myself.

Very quickly, my daze is surpassed by fear. I need help, but there's no one here. I am alone, just like I had planned. *What a genius.* My left arm is definitely broken. Not a clean break; there is no locus of pain, just a dull ache that soon becomes radiating misery. Although getting up is not a possibility, I have to make it to the phone. Scooching and slithering, I arrive at the wall phone, where my worst fears are realized: I can't reach the cord. When I shift my right glute to take pressure off of my throbbing left arm, I feel my cell phone, tucked in the rear pocket of my sweatpants.

I want to call Tracy, but I don't know if I should. She can't help me from Martha's Vineyard, and I don't want her to worry and freak out. I don't have the heart to call Schuyler. I know her so well; she will put this on herself. This is *my* mess—and no one is better at cleaning up my messes than Nina.

I dial, and wake her. "Nina, call the production office. Tell them I don't think I can make it today. Something's messed up."

She is still sleepy, but has a quick read on the problem. "I'm guessing you're symptomatic and you don't think your drugs are going to kick in." She assures me, "It'll be okay. We'll adjust your meds. You're going to be great today."

"No. I fell. I think I broke my arm. It's bad."

"Shit." Nina throws her jeans on over her pajamas, and she's in a taxi racing uptown within minutes of my call.

—

The time it takes for Nina to get to me, I put to good use, berating myself. I come close to crying. What stays the tears is my seething, self-directed anger. *Idiot. Do you realize what you've done? You screwed it all up. Your surgery, your health, the rehab, all the time and effort people put into you. Goddamn it, you just threw it all away.*

So many thoughts race through my head. *And what about the movie? I should be leaving in a few minutes for the set. What's Spike going to say? What will Stefon do—hire someone else, five minutes before crew call? This is a disaster. They're going to have to shut down today, and that's on me. So much is on me. How will Tracy and the kids feel? They've invested their love and attention in my recovery. Tracy toasted my determination to heal, and now I may have wrecked the whole thing. How could I be so selfish?*

My family has put up with so much crap. They've begged me to be careful, and I laughed it off. I may have done permanent damage to myself—not just to my arm; I may have hurt my spine. Four months since I had major back surgery, and I gambled my health and the security of my family, by being a fool.

Nina arrives and finds me, still on the floor. "Have you been down there the whole time?" she says, bending to help me up.

"Just don't touch my left arm. Don't even *say* 'left arm.'"

She looks at the appendage, misshapen and lifeless, and winces. "How's it look?" I ask.

She gently lifts me by the right arm into a chair. "I'm calling an ambulance."

"No," I protest. "No ambulance. I don't want to make a big deal out of this. We'll take a cab to the hospital." I shift, and my left elbow taps the back of the chair. The bolt of pain I experience is so searing, so profound, that my mother in Canada feels it. The noise this produces from me is appropriate to the occasion.

"I'm calling an ambulance," Nina repeats.

Now it all deteriorates into a fog of pain. I do remember two ridiculously good-looking EMTs showing up in my apartment, one female and one male, straight out of a Dick Wolf series. They ask if I want morphine. "Yes, please."

My next clear memory isn't until late that afternoon, as I'm wheeled out of surgery. A doctor, still in scrubs, approaches the gurney and looks into my squinting eyes. "Mr. Fox?"

I slowly nod. *I think so.*

"I'm Dr. Galatz, chief of orthopedic surgery here at Mount Sinai. I just fixed your arm."

I try to focus on her blurry form. "Was it bad?"

She smiles. "It wasn't good, but the surgery was successful. That arm is rebuilt to last."

She shows me a confusing picture of what looks like an erector set placed inside a limb. "What am I looking at?"

"That's an X-ray of your arm," she says, "with a stainless-steel plate and nineteen screws."

She calls it a spiral fracture of the humerus, which means the arm was twisted in the fall—like wringing a wet towel, only with bone and flesh. Shattered from shoulder to elbow, it took meticulous surgery, plus a half-pound of cutlery, to repair. As I will find out, a broken humerus is no fucking joke.

15

A WING AND A PROVERB

I wake up in another hospital room. I'm thinking about my phone call with Tracy last night. She had already spoken with the doctors, and Nina was keeping her up-to-date, so as usual, she was more informed about my situation than I was.

"We'll be there as soon as we can," she said. "Everyone is getting packed up. We're just waiting for a couple of seats to open up on tomorrow's flight."

"No, don't pack yet," I told her. "I think you should stay. You look forward to the Vineyard all winter, and the weather is supposed to be fantastic the rest of the week. Your mom's there. It's perfect. I don't want another one of my freakin' health crises to blow up one more family vacation. Stay; enjoy. Please. I'll see you and the girls in a few days."

The silence on the phone told me she still needed convincing.

"Honey, it's just a broken arm."

"It's a *badly* broken arm," she corrected me.

"Well, there's no such thing as a *goodly* broken arm." I heard a faint laugh. "Look, Nina is with me. Schuyler's coming to the hospital tomorrow.

The Schenkers promised to stop by. I'm golden. I love you. Go to the beach."

———

I get about eight hours of sleep, in two-hour intervals, during which time I'm stuck and re-stuck with needles, either repositioning the IV or drawing blood. Between the surgery in Baltimore and now this thing, over the last four months I've been jabbed so many times, my once-beautiful veins have been forced into hiding.

A nurse pushes the door open. "Good morning, Mr. Fox. How are you feeling?"

"Perforated."

"I brought you something."

The morphine hangover is making me goofy. "A blood pressure sleeve. I've always wanted one."

She holds up a magazine.

"I'm sorry, I can't see that without my glasses." She brings it closer. It's *People* magazine. On the cover: "Michael J. Fox & Tracy Pollan. Our 30-Year Love Story." I am intrigued. We did the interview with our friend Jess Cagle, along with a photo spread, in July. We even snuck Gus into a few shots. It's weird to see the finished product for the first time in this setting. It belongs in another life, a different world; a world in which Tracy and I are celebrities and we have a "Hollywood marriage." Actually, we live in New York, and when we're in L.A., we don't go anywhere near Hollywood; not even to visit my star on the sidewalk (which, if you're interested, is on Hollywood Boulevard, between La Brea and Highland).

At the moment, I'm not feeling the stardust. This is not a Hollywood moment. It's not my latest role (if it is, I'm going to fire my agent). It is strange to reconcile the shiny, happy persona staring out from the glossy cover of a magazine, with this busted lump of fifty-seven-year-old human, not gliding along a red carpet but lying in a hospital bed.

The nurse puts the magazine on the bedside table and goes about her routine, with a velocity born of skillful repetition. She comes at me with the blood pressure cuff, and swipes a thermometer wand across my forehead. As the sleeve tightens on my arm, I inquire, "What time is checkout?"

The machine reaches max pressure, gives a wheeze, and releases my arm. "You're staying at least another night."

"Two nights for a busted arm?"

She scribbles something on my chart, and answers, "I'm sure the doctor will go over the game plan, when she comes by after breakfast." The nurse turns to leave. "Any special food requests?"

"Edible would be fine. Thanks for the magazine," I say.

"Oh, that's mine. Could you please sign it before you leave?"

"Sure, no problem." I glance over at the magazine. Our thirtieth wedding anniversary was a month ago. We celebrated it, but didn't make a big deal out of the number, even though we were quietly impressed that we'd made it this far. It's funny, and a little ironic, that when we got married in front of close friends and family at a small country inn in Vermont, *People* panned our wedding. We had denied access to the magazine and all other media. Thirty years ago, pre-social media, pre-Instagram, pre-Twitter, pre-Facebook, we had a reasonable expectation that we could have an experience that was limited to just the people who were in that room. Frustrated by our refusal to offer up this private moment as a public spectacle, they projected the chaos outside the compound—crowds of onlookers, photographers, helicopters whirring above—to mean that our entire day, the ceremony and celebration afterward (all clear and precious memories), represented an epic fail by us. They said it was a complete fiasco; *nuptials in hell.*

The marriage was doomed.

We'll take the anniversary edition as a correction.

I'm soon confronted with a bowl of oatmeal, Jurassic raisins, and syrupy apple juice. I don't know where to start. "Thanks. I'll eat it later," I lie to the orderly. My goofiness is giving way to a mild but gathering sense of foreboding. I'm uneasy. Something has changed. I just haven't processed what it is yet.

I pick raisins out of the goo. Breakfast is over. As if on cue, Dr. Galatz and an associate stride in, accompanied by Nina. The doctor reintroduces herself. "Good morning. I'm Leesa Galatz. You may not remember meeting me yesterday . . ."

Surprisingly, I do recognize her as the orthopedic surgeon who performed the operation. "You showed me a picture of something. An X-ray."

"That's right. I emailed it to Nina, so you'll have it on file. A souvenir."

"Received," Nina says. And then to me, "It's horrifying."

Dr. Galatz carries on. "I've spoken with Dr. Theodore."

"He knows what happened?"

Nina says, "I called him yesterday, as soon as we got to the E.R., so I could connect him with the doctors here."

"I examined the site of the spinal surgery," Dr. Galatz says, "and told Dr. Theodore that I saw no signs of trauma or damage to the incision. It has healed nicely, so we are both confident that it's not a factor."

"So, in basic terms, my back is okay, then?"

"Your spine is fine," Dr. Galatz responds. "And your bones are strong, like a twenty-five-year-old's. But the impact was violent. A spiral fracture like yours will take time to heal, usually four to six weeks. We'll coordinate rehab with the folks at Johns Hopkins, to cover both issues. A physical therapist will come by your room later today to go through everything you'll need to do. Make sure you follow the instructions carefully."

Damn. More rehab. I'm going to need rehab from rehab.

She heads out the door. "I'll stop by again tomorrow."

"Looks like I'll be here," I say, without much enthusiasm.

Nina pulls out her phone. "Oh, before I forget, I called your brother Steve in Canada. I asked him to call your mom and let her know you're okay. You should text her, but I wouldn't include this . . ."

Nina taps her phone, pulls up the image from Dr. Galatz, and turns the screen toward me.

"God, that *is* horrifying," I concur.

"Creepy, right?"

A ghostly gray-and-black image, a skeletal arm, with multiple fractures up and down the bone, like fingers of lightning. It would shatter into a thousand pieces if not for those pins, and the plate anchoring the humerus to the shoulder. "And look at this!" She shows me another image on her phone. This one is more lurid, vivid and explicit. My first impression is *meat*. It's the exterior view, in living color: a long, jagged, nasty incision on my bruised and swollen left arm, since covered by layers of bandage and surgical tape, and hidden in a sling.

The injury to my arm will have consequences. Dr. Galatz tells me later that the stress of the orthopedic surgery alone will weaken me. My balance will be off; I'll have to reapproach walking, and prepare to learn a different set of skills to meet a new set of challenges. The work begins all over again.

I wasn't looking for another health problem, but one found me. So now I'm dealing with Parkinson's, a spinal condition, and a broken-down wing.

Every Picture Tells a Story

"I'm sorry. I should've stayed," Schuyler says.

In those desperate minutes I spent wallowing on the kitchen floor, I knew this would weigh heavily on Schuyler, whose reputation for compassion goes beyond the family, to school and her coworkers.

"Don't tell me if I was there, it still would've happened anyway," she insists.

"It would have," I counter.

"No, just by my being there, the timing would've been different."

I sit down in a hospital chair and guide Schuyler to sit across from me, on the foot of the bed. Wanting to avoid a prolonged rehashing of the butterfly effect, I assure her, "Then it would've been something else. I could've left the oven on, or tripped in the bathroom and cracked my head open on the sink. Things are going to happen."

She flops back on the bed and stares at the ceiling, her long hair spreading out over the hospital sheets. "I still think about what you went through in Baltimore, Dood. That was so disturbing. I wanted to help you, but I couldn't. I felt so powerless." She raises her head from the mattress.

"I know if I'd stayed with you Sunday night, I could've done something."

As I listen to Sky, I realize that she had witnessed the spectacle in Baltimore through the lens of a psychology major. She works with emotional issues on a daily basis, so she had a fair idea of what she was seeing. But more than that, I'm her father—and in both situations, her reaction was more visceral than clinical. She just wanted to protect me.

"You can't take this on, Schuyler. Honestly? I don't think I'm ever going to be truly safe. If I screw up, it's my mistake. I understand what you're feeling, but I swear to you, this had nothing to do with you not being there."

I read the doubt on her face. It suddenly occurs to me how wrong I had been to promise Tracy everything would be fine, because Schuyler was coming home with me. Unbelievably, to allay Tracy's fears about this New York trip, I used Schuyler as cover. I had every intention of being Mr. Independent.

I stand and cross over to my daughter.

"Look," I say. "I appreciate that your instinct was to stay and look out for me, because you know that I move too fast, and tend to be out of control. But I never should have put you in the position of having to protect me. This is on me, not on you."

My phone dings with an incoming text. "Curtis, Carolyn, and Ally are on their way up," I tell Sky. "They brought food." I catch her eye. "Are we okay?" She smiles and gives me a small thumbs-up. She's trying, a sweet gesture probably tinged with irony, but she commits to it.

"My thumb is up, too," I say. "You just can't see it."

———

Our good friends and traveling companions the Schenkers lighten the mood and rescue me from a dinner prepared in the hospital kitchen. It's a generous picnic: pasta, chicken parm, steak pizzaiola, and caprese salad. Carolyn reaches into an insulated bag and produces a dozen servings of Sant Ambroeus Italian ice creams. They are decadent and delicious. We inhale the gelato, while the girls entertain, singing along to Steve Winwood on Sky's iPhone speaker and dancing shuffle-step with my cane. Nina finds freezer space for the leftover ice cream, hopefully not with the plasma.

While he's the same age as me, and a perfectly healthy man, otherwise, Curtis is a bit of an accident-prone train wreck, himself: There were the two broken arms, flipping over the handlebars of a bike; the loss of his front teeth, from a fall while stepping out of the shower; and a torn Achilles tendon, playing tennis with his teenage son. There's more, but that's enough to make me feel better. He doesn't ask me how I broke my arm; he knows how this shit happens.

Ice cream and dancing are usually enough to keep me awake, but I'm fading fast, and they can all read it on my face. "Hey," I say, as they prepare to leave, "I have to show you something." I grab my iPhone and pull up the images from Dr. Galatz. Their eyes widen.

You can tell people about a personal malady or a major problem in your life, but it's not often that you can back it up with forensics. *This is what it is*. I don't have to explain it to you, or endeavor to make you feel what I feel. In the coming weeks, I will flash my X-ray to anyone and everyone—friends, family, hospital workers, random passers-by—and then double down with the full-color photo of my Frankenstein arm, with its eighteen-inch scar. Like an uncle with a cheap magic trick, it becomes my calling card. With these inside and outside images, you don't have to guess what's wrong with me.

This compulsive sharing of the X-ray is not really about my arm, at all. It's about Parkinson's.

As much I'd like to, it's not possible to sum up Parkinson's in a picture or two. I can't produce an X-ray. I can't show you the damage it's done. I have no photographic evidence of cell death or misfiring neurons. This personal quest to show people what's going on inside of me reveals a desire I had no previous way to satisfy.

It's a relief to be in a situation that I can explain with a picture.

Not coincidentally, the Foundation is working on a solution to this frustrating dilemma. The only X-ray we have for Parkinson's disease is *the patient*, and by extension, the PD community. We found that when patients meet, our conversation becomes a dialogue about symptoms and challenges, trying to triangulate what we learn from each other. Inspired by this, our Foundation launched an online program called "Fox Insight," to give patients a platform to share their lived experiences; it's a vehicle to express what we're feeling, give human shape to our disease. MJFF makes this valuable data available to scientists studying Parkinson's.

It has fired up the patient community; fifty thousand have participated so far. We believe the accumulated results of "Fox Insight" will help people see not just a snapshot of Parkinson's, but the big picture we're trying to develop.

An X-ray illustrates an injury, but it can also offer proof of repair. Everyone in this war on PD wants to pull that photo up on our iPhones.

My Sincere Regrets

Leaving the hospital today, I'm feeling curiously low. Nina handles the details of my discharge. We're accompanied by my old friend Belinda, who will help with the transfer. This stay should've been easier than Baltimore. I'm only a few blocks from home, so the close proximity allows for drop-ins by friends and family: Sky, of course; George and Harlan; Will, the therapist; all of my doctors; and the Schenkers. But the more love and attention they all shower on me, the more detached I begin to feel.

Physically, I'm fine. I'm not terribly symptomatic. No pain in my arm. But I am emotionally diminished, as if something is incomplete. Ahead of me lies a battle, but I have no clue as to what weapons I'll need. Moreover, I feel guilty. My head is full of the faces and names of the people I've let down. There really is a butterfly effect; one small incident, one tiny insignificant event, can have a reverberating effect on the future. You make a sloppy turn into a doorway, and everything changes. You position your arm to break a fall, and it impacts countless lives. A scene in a movie doesn't get shot. A vacation is cut short. Hours of physical therapy go to waste.

And on it goes.

＝

We're home. Nina opens the door to the empty apartment. Belinda slowly guides me down the hallway, toward the den. As we pass the kitchen door, I avoid looking in at the scene of the crime. Nina follows, and I ask her to get Dr. Theodore on the phone.

I swallow hard. "Hey, Doc," I say.

With a friendly "Hey, Mike," he asks me how I'm feeling. I don't hear the words or the tone. I launch right into my mea culpa.

"I screwed up. And I'm so sorry."

Generously, he reminds me that it was an accident, and accidents happen. *Yeah, a lot.* He confirms that no damage was done to my spine. "You sure messed up your arm, though." He does not sugarcoat what is to come. "This is going to be difficult. It's going to set you back a bit. With your arm in a sling, your balance will be thrown off. It will take time to regain your walking, but with therapy and patience, you'll get it done."

I sink further into my chair, careful to adjust for my goddamn sling.

Dr. Theodore continues, "I recommended to Tracy that you have round-the-clock aides with you again. It won't be for as long this time, but just until you are capable of moving safely, with the arm out of commission. And you absolutely cannot fall. I'm not worried about the spine; by now, that's fully fused and difficult to injure. But there's lots of stuff to break, and you don't want to break any of it."

I am numb. He had me at "round-the-clock aides."

———

Just two days ago, I awoke in this same room, feeling liberated. For the first time in months, no one was hovering nearby, watching, anticipating, commenting. At last, I was out from under the suffocating dome of that surveillance. I'd later see a Showtime series, *Escape at Dannemora*, which reminded me of this feeling. A true story, two convicts aspire to escape an upstate New York penitentiary. Benicio del Toro and Paul Dano sneak out of their respective cells and meet several levels below, in the building's sub-basement. They're plotting to use sewage tunnels to reach freedom. It's dark and eerily quiet. They look at each other. Benicio asks Paul how long he has been in prison. "Fourteen years," he replies. Benicio points out that this is the first time in fourteen years that no one knows where the hell he is.

I could relate. This was the first time, in a very long time, that no one was with me or watching me. I guess I answered the eternal question: *If Mike fell in the kitchen and no one was there to see him, would he still break his arm?*

It's not that I *tried* to hurt myself; it's that I didn't try hard enough *not* to hurt myself. It was hubris. Unfettered pride. And you know what pride goeth before . . .

Actually, you may not. The precise wording of the Proverb is: *Pride goeth before destruction, and an haughty spirit before a fall.* As bad as the break is, I wouldn't call it destruction, though my pride did seem to manifest as a haughty spirit. That's Bible-speak for showing off.

———

Counterintuitively, Parkinson's and the tumor on my spine were easier to accept than the broken arm. They had been there for years; stealthy and insidious, they crept up on me. The arm crisis was there in an instant, an explosion. A cataclysm.

I am unprepared for the fallout. My mood darkens. Even with all my health issues, I don't believe I've ever fully grasped the very real depression and marginalization experienced by many who are ill and suffering. Measured on the misery index, the sum total of my afflictions barely nudges the needle on the lower end of the scale, when compared to the pain and hardship of so many people in this world. Their burdens exist on levels I can't even imagine: the death of a child; the loss of liberty; the exile from home or country. There is no end to sadness.

But we can only live our own lives. In my life, at this moment, I am stretched by what I have to deal with. I'm at a new place, with new thoughts. I'm thinking about my messed-up balance and all the rest of it—a very real setback for me. Now I've been pelted with too many lemons to even think about lemonade. It's like Tracy finding me on the couch all those years ago, sleeping off a drinking binge; I am bored with it. Bored with myself. Bored with this whole situation.

There is no way to put a shine on my circumstance, as I have so many times in the past, publicly and privately. Positivism is a state of mind one achieves, and I am presently an underachiever.

Have I oversold optimism as a panacea, commodified hope? Have I been an honest broker with the Parkinson's community? The understanding I've reached with Parkinson's is sincere, but the expression of it risks being glib. I have made peace with the disease, and I might have presumed that others had, too. In telling other patients, "Chin up! It will be okay!" did I look to them to validate my optimism? Is it because I needed to believe it myself? Things don't always turn out. Sometimes things turn shitty. I have to tell people the whole deal.

This brings me to an inflection point. Over the coming months, I will feel a shift in my worldview, and struggle to believe in ideas that I've espoused for years. Have I reached a line beyond which there is no compromise or consolation?

My optimism is suddenly finite.

16

HOMELAND SECURITY

Everything begins again; same thing, only different. New aides are hired, for what the doctors assure me will be a shorter stint in my home. Clara, my daytime aide, exudes an Irish affability, but is nevertheless strictly by the book. Her nighttime counterpart, Brigid, I can tell right away is a character, but still focused and vigilant. Do they see me as a Parkinson's patient with a broken arm, or—as I see myself—as a guy with a broken arm who happens to have Parkinson's? Either way, they have their marching orders: No risky behaviors that could result in a fall. This time, I'm with the program, all the way. I have a new, painful understanding of the consequences, and a willingness to accept whatever precautions are imposed.

My family lineage can be described as Anglo-Irish-Canadian. My Belfast-born grandmother was a major influence in my life, so I find the brogues of my new health aides to be sentimentally familiar. Clara's may be one or two decibels louder than it needs to be; her daily "Good morning, Michael!" resonates through the door, down the hallway, and from room to room, waking everyone in the house. She is perfectly suited to "rise and shine" daytime duties. Brigid is a little softer-spoken. Both women hail from Galway, but their accents are slightly different; if Clara's sings, Brigid's crackles, slices and rises at the tail of the final syllable, as if she is in a constant state of dubiousness. If I swing my feet around from the bed and onto the floor with no obvious purpose, Brigid quickly reacts, "And where do you think you're going?" It is like hearing Nana's voice across time. Perhaps in answer to both of them, I swing my feet back onto the bed and mumble, "Nowhere."

For a nighttime nurse, not sleeping is part of the job. Still, Brigid has less activity to observe, so on the nights when I can't get comfortable and fall asleep, I turn on the TV to search for something we'll both like. One of our favorites is *The Great British Baking Show*. It's the kind of television you can talk through—and Brigid can talk. We swap stories; Brigid's are longer and more picaresque than mine. When I show her my osteo-porn—the infamous X-ray with the metal plate and the screws— she recounts how they dealt with broken limbs when she was a girl. "We'd send for the bonesetter." In the absence of a local doctor, a bonesetter, a tinker, really, would show up with his cart equipped with a set of instruments, to fix any orthopedic injury a villager might sustain.

"Sorry, Brigid, but your bonesetter sounds a tad barbaric."

"Nah," she protests. "He often did a bang-on job. Although occasionally, horribly disfiguring." She'd see a neighbor hobbling across the road, and she'd know right away whose handiwork she was looking at.

Sometimes the subject turns to travel. Brigid expresses regret that she's never journeyed to another country or state; just dozens of round trips between Dublin and New York. She has a longing, a stuck-in-the-mud feeling. My health issues, physically and lately psychologically, have brought me to a similar place. I have a longing to be free of this medical Skinner box. "So," I ask Brigid, "if you could go anywhere on the planet, where would you go? Where would your dreams take you?"

She closes her eyes and with a wistful smile, says, "The Grand Canyon."

Yeah, I think, *the Grand Canyon. Good choice. Beautiful, mysterious, scary around the edges.*

Sam and I stopped at the Grand Canyon twenty years ago, part of a father-son cross-country trip. One afternoon we sat at the trailhead and watched tourists saunter down to the canyon floor, totally unprepared for the long, hot crawl back up in the mid-day Arizona sun; no hats, no water bottles. Some even carried ice cream cones.

"Go to the Grand Canyon; it's excellent. Take your kids, take your husband." *Bring hats; hydrate; skip the ice cream.*

"Nah," she replies with a shake of her head. "They won't go. The kids are too old, and my fella is happy at home."

"Then *you* should go."

Although I encourage Brigid to follow her bliss, the only traveling I can do, at the moment, is in my mind, and mostly to places I've already been: Thailand, India, especially Bhutan. I'm discouraged from even considering future voyages. Tracy keeps talking about Africa, but I'm not sure I'll be able to travel at all. It's hard to feel aspirational when so much is unknown. And not just travel: family events, day-to-day life, acting a couple of times a year. I just don't know.

———

My quandary is not abstract or philosophical. It's real. Sometimes I wobble—it may look like I'm about to fall, but it's just a wobble. I'm finding my balance. My mind and my body are making the correction together. But people just can't help themselves. They have an atavistic response to any aberrant motion. If I catch my toe on the carpet and trip, immediately someone shouts, "Be careful!" *I am being careful, and it's too late, anyway.* Their advice is well-intentioned, but I feel a subtle shaming. As if my goal is to trip and break my other arm. It hits me like the "Did I do this to myself?" guilt that I worked through after my Parkinson's diagnosis.

That shame is visiting me again.

What do I want from my world right now? To accept work without creating contingencies or fire escapes. To cross a threshold and turn the corner without any drama. To hear Esmé's voice in the hallway, and go to wherever she is, without its being a big production. To get a popsicle, when I want a popsicle, and not wait for someone to bring it to me.

———

A few weeks pass. I'm stable enough to carry on without the home health aides. They are not so different from the crew that preceded them, but there's just something about these two Irish women that makes it hard to say goodbye. They allowed this recuperation to be a little more bearable. On their way out the door, I give gifts. For Clara—a bottle of Irish whiskey. For Brigid—the biggest goddamn Grand Canyon coffee-table book I can find.

Inside My Head and Out of My Mind

A broken arm heals relatively quickly, especially when Dr. Galatz is the local bonesetter. The spinal injury took its time to heal; Parkinson's can't be healed at all. As usual, my focus is on the corporeal, and through physical therapy, my body is better. But I don't *feel* better. My spirit lags behind. The violence of the fall, and breaking my arm, dropped me into a semi–fugue state.

Now, as autumn sets in, I must slowly rejoin my life. It's time to understand my circumstances more clearly.

I try not to get too New Age-y. I don't talk about things being "for a reason." But I do think that the more unexpected something is, the more there is to learn from it. In my case, I have to examine the hard truth: *What made me skip down the hallway to the kitchen, as if it was all fine, when I'd been in a wheelchair six weeks earlier?* My attitude was cavalier, in line with my optimism. I had certain expectations, validated by past results, that every-thing would work out okay. But there had been failures in the past, too. And I realize now that I hadn't given the failures equal weight.

Clearly, my embrace of fate needs some retooling. A strong instinct, an inner voice, is telling me: *Don't waste this opportunity. Don't blow this.* For years, my body has demanded all of the attention. It's time to put some serious thought into my mind.

17

HEAD GAMES

The artist/activist Anna Deavere Smith defines herself as a "hopeaholic." Save me a seat at the next meeting: *My name is Michael, and I am an optimist.* But seriously, if optimism is my faith, I fear I'm losing my religion.

This is a new kind of thinking for me. Can you be an optimist and a realist at the same time? Or does that add up to stoicism? Not that I put on a brave face, or that I'm courageous, for that matter. I am not a hero. Sure, I've been through some ordeals, tough times. But I always managed to accept life on life's terms, and up to this point, I found those terms acceptable. I was able to take on whatever came my way, forge through it, no matter what. Now my attempt to make any sense of it leaves me feeling indifferent. I'm numb. Weary. Optimism, as a frame of mind, is not saving me.

Much of what is important in my life grew out of my optimism: embarking on my career, getting married, having children. Another example, The Michael J. Fox Foundation for Parkinson's Research, was once just a hopeful idea, a vision we aspired to make real. We didn't wonder if it would be successful; we just accepted that it would have to be. We didn't force our vision into an existing paradigm, but let it evolve, seeking niches and fissures in the neuro-research landscape, reimagining what a world without Parkinson's would look like. Powered by our good intentions, the few of us who were there at the beginning would spout our mantra for the project: *purity of motive*. Find a way to relieve symptoms, halt progression, discover a cure, and solve PD.

Optimism and idealism, tempered with realism. To succeed, we'd have to put hard work behind our hopefulness.

This level of positivism used to define me; all scenarios were best-case. So why has a broken arm scrambled all my coordinates? What should qualify as the least of my problems has become greater than all others. What is it that perverts the scale? My arm has been out of the sling for weeks, but my ass is still in it.

I feel like, *Enough already*. I can't just stamp it with a happy face and put it in the out-box. The immediacy of the situation calls for fluid thinking, but my mind is muddy. I enter a period of idleness, time that could be spent seeking answers. Instead, I seek a time-out.

Eventually, I will take the advice of my friend George Stephanopoulos and try Transcendental Meditation. But in the short term, it will be TV over TM.

But First, Avoid

"Sometimes you're ahead and sometimes behind." That's how Ralph Ellison's Invisible Man described the difficulty in following the complicated jazz beats of a Louis Armstrong record. That's how I feel about time with my family. I can't always go where they go, when they go there. My participation is syncopated. I want to be a companion, not a responsibility—or worse, a liability. By just showing up, I provide an X factor that can drastically alter their experience. So I pick my moments: when to join in, and when to stay home.

I try to spend alone time productively—reading books, attending to Foundation and other work-related projects, and catching up on email. Or . . . I can get sucked into the vortex of cable television, Apple TV, and the panoply of streaming platforms. Too often, I choose TV. It's an easy escape, comforting. It doesn't require input, or even full attention. Best of all, I don't have to move. I haven't fallen off the couch once.

As for my viewing preferences, generally I program my remote control to bounce between news on MSNBC (I find that Rachel Maddow is smarter than me), and ESPN (whoever is running, jumping, skating, or tossing a ball). When I tire of this fare, my remote takes me into the far reaches of the channel listings, on the hunt for something to occupy my time.

My current bingeing habits reflect my state of mind. Hunter S. Thompson observed that "When the going gets weird, the weird turn pro." During my time as a shut-in, I discover a treasure trove of professional weirdness, starting with BUZZR, a station that exclusively broadcasts vintage game shows. It has to be a cheap way to fill air time; most of the participants are dead, and I don't think their heirs are rolling in residuals. There's the late Steve Allen on *What's My Line?*, inventing the question "Is it bigger than a bread box?" The late Richard Dawson licking strangers on the original *Family Feud*. *Match Game*'s Gene Rayburn (deceased), asking hypothetical double entendre questions, referencing characters like "Dumb Dora" and "Fat Freddy." It's every bit as brainless as it sounds, yet, as a diversion, it has its merits. Absurd can be fantastic, as long as we agree that it's absurd.

I watch grittier absurd stuff, too. I often tune in to the Heroes & Icons network, with its library of old TV Westerns that aired slightly before I was born. My dad used to call them "horse operas" or "oaters." Now here they are, galloping across my giant seventy-five-inch screen in all of their crisp black-and-white glory.

In the early morning, once I'm awake, Parkinson's keeps me awake. *A shaky man gets no rest.* I turn on my flat-screen buddy and I am mesmerized, lulled into a stupor. The rodeo kicks off at 5 a.m., with Clint Walker as *Cheyenne.* At 6:00, *Maverick.* Then *blam! blam!* Two half-hour episodes of *Wanted Dead or Alive,* with Steve McQueen. My mom says she was watching this Western when she went into labor with me. She refused to be taken to the hospital until the end of the episode. *Way to go, Mom.* At 8:30: *Have Gun—Will Travel,* with its killer theme song "The Ballad of Paladin."

These old shows from the Eisenhower era are nostalgic, and that can be either positive or negative; while they're funny and entertaining, they can also be grossly politically incorrect. The bottom line is, I find these shows distracting, a temporary diversion from my malaise, a swinging gold watch in the hands of a hypnotist.

Look at Me, I'm on TV

I'm not just a bystander. Although I came in later, I occupy my own place in the pendulous arc of television history, as Alex Keaton, a high-energy young Republican with a serious man-crush on Ronald Reagan. *Family Ties* was like the programs I've been sampling lately, wholly and completely of its time. Occasionally, we tapped into the national zeitgeist and dealt with heavier issues (drug abuse, teen suicide, marital problems), while cringing at the likelihood that the NBC announcer would promote these as "very special episodes." We figured our audience would decide for themselves what was special, and what wasn't. We were just amazed that so many fans tuned in every week.

President Ronald Reagan was, in fact, a big fan. The one-time TV horse opera star (*Death Valley Days*) claimed that *Family Ties* was his favorite show, probably due to the fact that Alex's character was such a Reagan devotee. One day our executive producer, Gary Goldberg, received a call from the White House: The press office was lobbying for the Gipper to appear on the show. Now, that would've been a "very special episode"; but Gary, the writers, and I were unanimous that the president could guest on the show *only* if he attended the Monday-morning script reading; rehearsals throughout the week; Thursday camera blocking; the Friday-night show, taped live before a studio audience; curtain call and cast cheers; plus late-night pick-ups. As it turned out, we weren't *that* special.

This process—the first look at each week's script; getting the show on its feet (so to speak); starting to block the scenes on the set; developing the story and inspiring the writers to make it tighter and funnier; locking in the camera moves; and finally, presenting the results to the audience—was a supreme example of optimism in action. No matter how the week unfolded, it was never a question that it would be our funniest episode yet. That was always our default objective: *Just be funny.*

The audience who grew up with us are now in their forties and fifties. The "hippie-era parents with yuppie-era children" plotline isn't so relatable to today's audience, who barely remember President Obama, never mind Presidents Reagan or Nixon. But I'd like to think that young viewers in the 2020s might stumble on Alex Keaton and the Keaton family of Columbus, Ohio, and if they're not too distracted, just laugh.

Reagan Redux

Unlike Alex Keaton, my politics couldn't be further from Ronald Reagan's, but he became somewhat of a presence in my life and career. Apart from his affinity for *Family Ties*, he was the subject of a very funny shout-out in *Back to the Future.*

DOC
Then tell me, Future Boy.
Who's President of the United States in 1985?

MARTY

Ronald Reagan.

DOC

Ronald Reagan? The actor? Who's Vice President, Jerry Lewis?

In 1986, Ronald Reagan invited me to a State Dinner at the White House. Being a Democrat, I hesitated, but then I thought about it for a while. As ironic as it is to say these days, I had respect for the office. I considered it an honor. As it turned out, he was a genial and welcoming host.

Years later, Nancy Reagan even joined our Foundation in the pro-science side of the stem-cell debates. It was not the conservative position, so a bit of a surprise. People are not always as advertised.

Advertisers, however, know who their people are. We are what we watch—and the commercials slotted into our favorite programs can be revelatory. I turn on a football game, and it sells me beer and trucks; switch to MTV, and I'm in a world of condoms and Clearasil. The strange television landscape that I currently occupy is dotted with commercials—not for coffee, or cars, or Burger King—but for products targeted to geriatrics. Walk-in tubs, the Acorn Stairlift, reverse mortgages, portable oxygen units, catheters that are—get this—*nearly* pain-free, and the ever-popular adult diapers. *Oh my god, is* this *my demographic?* From now on, I can look forward to early-bird dinners and discounts on movie tickets. Sure, I like a good nap now and then, but I'm not ready for a dirt nap.

Maybe I'm just straddling the void; I'm probably the only person who has been featured on the cover of *Rolling Stone* and *AARP* in the same year. After all, I'm almost fifty-eight. That's the average age of diagnosis for a Parkinson's patient, so by that metric, I've been fifty-eight for twenty-nine years. That makes me eighty-seven.

This is how my mind isn't working.

I'm living the life of a retired person, a decade too soon. My world is contracting, not expanding. In terms of the space-time continuum, I'm closer to my exit than to my entrance point.

My fascination with vintage TV has something to do with the fact that I decide when I want to be in that world, and not in the present. I slip into another reality. It's one of the million iterations of time travel—to visit a world that's pre-me. My time hadn't begun, and therefore it hadn't begun to run out. And just like the performers in these old shows, someday I will survive myself in reruns.

18

MARYLAND, MY MARYLAND

Light rain, heavy traffic. We're nearing the two-hour mark of what promises to be a four-hour drive from Baltimore back to New York. Nina is piloting the SUV, just as she had from New York to Baltimore earlier this morning. This day has been circled in red on the calendar for months: Dr. Theodore had scheduled a follow-up MRI on my spine, six months after the surgery. The results would reveal if the procedure had been successful: if there had been any regrowth of the tumor, or re-impingement on the spinal cord.

Going into today's test, I'll admit to a degree of anxiety. Normally I could bluff my way through it, relying on an old standby axiom: "If you imagine the worst-case scenario, and it actually happens, you've lived it twice." It didn't ring true this time. I wasn't imagining things. What I was feeling was fear. Not frozen-in-my-tracks, don't leave my room, don't make eye contact terror, but legitimate fear of a negative result. I had already lived it, and had no desire to live it again. If these films showed regrowth of the mass, or deterioration of my spine, I was screwed.

At the halfway point of our return journey, Nina wisely pulls into one of those generic, one-on-either-side-of-the-turnpike mini-malls, basically life support systems for cavernous toilet facilities. I stumble out of the car and into the building. I'm wearing sweatpants, a green-checked flannel shirt, two weeks of stubble, and an aggressively unkempt head of hair. I blend right in. Clumsily, I make my way through the crowd of fellow travelers, stabbing at the floor with my four-pronged HurryCane.

After the restroom, I make a beeline for the Cinnabon concession. I select the sleeve of four minis, figuring I'll have at least three opportunities to "Just Say No" and show my arteries mercy.

I lean against a pillar, a few steps away from Nina, who's waiting to buy some candy from the newsstand, which is temporarily shuttered. The Cinnabon lady says that the cashier is on minute four of a five-minute break.

As I wait, my mind is processing and analyzing the day's events. I convinced the anesthesiologist to employ a lighter touch, and without the heavy sedative, I somehow managed to remain still during the MRI. Shaking off only a mild Valium hangover, I think about the significance of Dr. Theodore's reading of the results.

Tracy stayed in New York to attend Esmé's swim meet, the kind of event I miss on a regular basis because of my freakin' health issues. Dr. Theodore had spoken to my wife on the phone the moment I was out of the machine, so she already knew the outcome. We'd have a lot to talk about when I got home.

After almost forty years in the public eye, I am acutely aware of being observed. A slow pan to my right, and sure enough, about ten feet away, a guy stands eyeballing me. I'm guessing he's talking himself into coming over to say hi, or to get a selfie.

And here he comes, a big guy, 6' 2" maybe, short black hair with a six o'clock shadow, in jeans and a work coat. He'd be intimidating if it wasn't for his eyes . . . they're light, bright, and disarming.

"Are you Michael J. Fox?"

I nod.

"Oh, wow," he says. "I'm binge-watching every episode of *Spin City*."

"Thanks," I say. He glances down at my cane and back up again. "I'm sorry about your . . ."

Suddenly I feel the need to explain. "I had back surgery . . ." *Am I really going to go through the whole thing with this guy?*

Then he saves me: "I'm ex-military. I'm being treated for depression—PTSD—for a while now. It's going well, really good."

"That's great," I say, happy to be talking about him.

"I just wanted to tell you that, because, you know, you've helped me a lot."

He didn't want anything, this gentle giant. He just wanted to give me something—and it was beyond valuable. "I'm glad," I say. "What's your name?"

"Derek."

Nina shows up with her candy. I say goodbye to Derek, shake his hand, and he watches me limp-shuffle off. I'll bet he's thinking: *I feel better than Michael J. Fox looks.*

Back in the car, I fluff my pillow, ready to nap all the way to Manhattan. My mom will be visiting us soon from Vancouver. I look forward to telling her the news. It's official: The surgery took. The tumor is not growing back. The spinal cord is free and clear. It couldn't have gone better.

I think about the encounter with Derek. It stirred a feeling of gratitude: that through my example of living with adversity, I was able to positively affect someone else's life.

Another feeling remains, however. No matter how I try to suppress it, there's a lingering fear.

I sleep, though not well.

19

THE ONLY THING TO FEAR

I have at least two things in common with Franklin Delano Roosevelt: 1) the covert use of a wheelchair, and 2) a fear of fear.

"The only thing we have to fear is fear itself." Those words rallied a nation worn down by the starkness of the Depression, and FDR's message has led me through some dark times. I've always been moved by that speech; I draw inspiration from it. It's not that I'm fearless: I fear terrorist attacks, earthquakes, Black Widow spiders, losing track of my kids late at night, and a thousand other dreaded possibilities. I just don't fear those things *now*, in this moment, because there is no reason to. They're not a present reality. I'm not afraid of what might happen, in the same way I fear something that's certain to occur. Even so, in the last year, I have truly begun to experience the terrible binding power of "fear itself."

Just as Queen Elizabeth proclaimed 1992 her "annus horribilis," I would call my 2018 a terrible, horrible, no good, very bad year. Physically difficult and emotionally challenging, the pain worsened; the repeated falls became more dangerous; the resulting injury, disastrous. We lost Tracy's father, a mentor and beloved friend. The events of 2018 have been a crucible: a gauntlet I needed to walk, or, more precisely, learn to walk.

After such a strange year, it seems completely surreal to think I might be closing it out on a safari. Who am I kidding? Am I up to this?

My family has planned a trip to Africa, spanning the last ten days of December. I've always been drawn to this kind of adventure travel; still, I have some perfectly rational misgivings. I'm concerned not only that I won't be able to do much trekking, I don't know if my receptors are open to taking in this experience. I'm tempted by the fact that some of our favorite traveling companions are joining the trip; the Stephanopoulii and the Schenkers, two families who are accustomed to my particular challenges. Tracy keeps stressing to me: "You'll be in the jeep thingy all day. You won't have to walk anywhere, and the lodging is all on ground level. It's perfect."

I peruse the travel materials. "It isn't going to be like Disneyland, is it? With giraffes planted outside the hotel window?"

"It's a real safari," Tracy promised.

Sam comes at it from a different angle. "We all want you to be there, Pops." He invokes a joke I'd told him twenty years earlier, when, nervous and unsure, he first went to summer camp. Foolishly, I thought this would make him feel better: "Remember, if you and a buddy are hiking in the woods and a bear starts chasing you, you don't have to outrun the bear; you just have to outrun your buddy."

Sure enough, Sam makes the callback. "Remember," Sam says, "if we're out on the savanna and a lion starts to chase us, we don't have to outrun the lion. . . ."

"Dad jokes? You come at me with Dad jokes?"

"We can outrun you, Pops. I'm just saying."

The callback would prove prescient.

In the days leading up to the departure for Africa, my family, our friends, and their kids dial up their anticipation. I am happy that my presence isn't mandatory—they are all going, with or without me. But I am somewhat cheered that they'd rather I be there.

If only to avoid FOMO, I decide it is worth it to drag my beleaguered body halfway across the world to the savannas of Tanzania. What it comes down to, finally, is Tracy's confidence that I'll be able to handle whatever comes (or charges) my way.

Leopardspotting

The first leopard we see is impressive. Twenty feet above, ensconced in a fig tree, a large male is camouflaged to perfection, his rosettes melding with the dappled sunlight that filters through the leaves. If Seurat had painted this scene pointillistically, he would have created his first photo-realistic work of art. I somehow find the cat's eyes, squinting until the dots connect so I can fully appreciate his languorous form. His dead prey, a young antelope, is safely wedged into a fork in the bough. He is cleaning his victim, licking the hair off before he rips into the meat. I recognize this behavior from hours of watching "Big Cat Diary" on *Animal Planet*. The leopard's head lolls forward and his gaze seems to meet mine. I'll admit to an *Oh, shit* moment, but I understand that he isn't sizing me up for a meal; he has already brought lunch home. Besides, one of mankind's key defenses against being eaten is that we just aren't that delicious. Even so, this master predator could abandon his arboreal lair and go from descent, to pounce, to dispatching me with a bite to the neck in less than three seconds.

If I wandered the savanna alone and on foot, this might be the outcome, but it's not going to happen today. I'm taking in this tableau from the safety of a safari-outfitted Range Rover. One of a convoy of three, it is occupied by me, Tracy, and our four kids, Sam, twenty-nine, Aquinnah and Schuyler, twenty-three, and Esmé, seventeen. The other two cars hold George

Stephanopoulos, Ali Wentworth, and their two teenage girls, Elliott and Harper; and Curtis and Carolyn Schenker and their three, all young adults, Ally, Brad, and Jack. The seemingly haphazard formation, like patrol cars at a crime scene, is actually strategic positioning: We're surrounding the leopard tree on three sides.

Awestruck by our daring proximity to one of Africa's Big Five game animals, we allow a small amount of nervous chatter. The situation doesn't feel dangerous to me, though the vehicles wouldn't impress anyone as leopard-proof, as they are completely open on both sides, noisy, and clumsy on the getaway. The guides explain that it's our collective enormity that protects us—as long as we stay in the vehicles, the leopard doesn't recognize a group of humans; rather, he regards each truck as a single entity, a giant monolithic beast, too big to mess with. Still, the guides emphasize again and again: Never leave the vehicle. If you do, you will break the shape, spoil the illusion, and expose the fraud. You are separate and vulnerable, and seconds away from adorning the limb of a fig tree.

No Time to Wallow

There are two outings a day—one in the morning, from sunrise to noon, when it becomes too hot to remain on the savanna; and a second sortie in the late afternoon to evening, returning back to camp shortly after sunset. On the second afternoon, we have a smaller group, just two vehicles: George and his family in one, me and mine in the other. A sudden torrential downpour convinces the Stephs to head back to camp. But my family and our guide opt to wait out the rain, finding cover in a thicket around a small watering hole. The skies clear and we shed our rain ponchos, setting off again after a herd of elephants reported to be in the area.

After observing the pachyderms—about twenty of them, infants to elder males—we give wide berth to a seething mass of Cape buffalo. Seeing this tsunami of beef, we are in awe. Lumbering yet somehow spritely, the buffalo seem to be forming in lines, like battalions preparing for battle. I jokingly mention this to my guide, Abraham, who gives me a look and says, "Exactly." Putting the bulls out front and the younger males in the second line creates an interior safe zone for the cows and calves.

Tracy asks, "Who are they going to attack?"

The guide laughs. "Us."

"Seriously?" I say.

"Don't worry. The jeep can outrun them."

"What if the jeep breaks down?" I ask logically.

That was my turn to be prescient.

As the sun sets, we retrace our tracks, skirting the watering hole where we had sheltered from the downpour. The closer to the watering hole, the more viscous the earth becomes. Soon, we are spinning our wheels, deeper and deeper into an inescapable ooze. A large fig tree attracts my attention, eerily similar to the leopard tree from the previous day. The sun is low on the western horizon. No light dapples this leopard tree, which lurks as an ominous silhouette backlit by a red streak. A cacophony of birdcalls, animal grunts, and frog rantings grows louder as the light ebbs.

The kids seem weirdly unconcerned that there might be something spying on us from the boughs.

Tracy, to my surprise, also exudes confidence that we will soon be on our way back to camp. However, Abraham discovers that the winch he carries in the back of the truck is broken. The radio works only intermittently. Even if he could reach someone, it could take an hour for them to locate and liberate us.

While we consider our situation, I recall that savanna watering holes are killing grounds, where predators rush in and eviscerate helpless prey: those who can't quickly escape, who wouldn't put up much of a fight; the young, the sick, the lame, and the old. I tick off the last three boxes (self-identifying as "old" is new for me, but there it is).

I have the irrational thought that I should volunteer to remain behind while the guide, flashlight in one hand, pistol in the other, leads my family to safety. After all, I'd only slow down their escape. At the same time, it occurs to me that left behind in the sinking vehicle, by the watering hole, in the dark, I'd just be waiting to get picked off.

I'm not a panicky guy. Given my circumstances, I handle oncoming traffic as calmly and deftly as the next person. But lately, I have become increasingly prone to a sort of free-floating anxiety, which surely has to do with the physical and emotional assault I experienced over this last year. Now, in our drama by the watering hole, my anxiety is no longer free-floating, but firmly attached to a fear of being bear-bait. If my family and I are being chased by a leopard, they don't have to outrun the leopard, they just have to outrun me—which they could do at a brisk walk. If you imagine the worst-case scenario as being attacked by a leopard, and it actually happens . . . well, you get it.

At last, Abraham raises a radio reply from a passing vehicle, a rival safari company. They show up and, in short order, with a functioning winch, release us from the muck. It is a surprisingly brief but deeply appreciated drive back to our little settlement at the plain's edge.

The leopard from the previous day hadn't scared me. It was the leopard in the tree at twilight—the one that I *didn't* see, the one that probably wasn't even there—that scared me stupid.

Night Tripping

After a fine meal, we enjoy a performance by a local dance troupe, who manage to get everyone up and stomping and flailing. I take a pass, but George surprises all of us with some good moves. With the final flickering of what our camp master, Lazarus, calls "bush TV"—the crackling campfire at the center of our small village of canvas tents—each family makes their way back to their respective shelters. We bunk along family lines; there are tents for the adults, and separate tents for the kids.

What awaits me is more frightening than a whole tent full of leopards. This is where the real fear kicks in. It's not the tent itself, which is well lit and quite inviting; a large canvas structure complete with an improbable four-poster bed. While spacious, it seems somewhat cluttered with assorted colonial furniture and Africanalia. It's easy to navigate now, but once the lights are out, the tent becomes a minefield.

Owing to my age (there it is again), and to an extent, my recent injuries and longstanding disability, I tend to visit the bathroom once or twice during the night. At home, I'm of course familiar with the terrain from bed to bathroom, and slowly and somewhat shakily make my way safely to and from each time. I lean on walls, doing what my occupational therapist calls "furniture surfing": reaching out and touching furniture along one's path, not so much for support as for relativity of space. At home, I leave the bathroom light on dim, which creates a target for me to lurch toward. But here, on this moonless night, the only illumination is provided by two tiny pinpoints on either side of my head. Strapped to my forehead, my "hands-free-best-for-bed-reading-flexible-arm-book-light" makes me look like a fish out of water, specifically, a prehistoric anglerfish from the Mariana Trench, that has somehow flopped its way to the plains of Africa.

These nightly trips are by far the most dangerous and potentially fatal activities I'll engage in during all of my time in Tanzania. On my journey across the tent floor, I take pains not to trip over a chair, or reach out to touch a rickety tea table. Chances are good I'd do a face-plant into a gazelle-horn hat rack, or forget myself and lean against the "wall," which is merely fortified canvas. I could bring the whole tent down on top of me and my sleeping wife. Should any of these mishaps occur and I break a bone, crack my skull, or god forbid, injure Tracy in some way, we are hours away from any help or medical services.

Fraidy-Cat

These three vignettes from my trip to Africa represent three fears that res-
onate through every phase of life. There's the leopard in the tree, viewed
from an armada of SUVs: a real danger, but it's contained, and if you're
careful, you will survive it, maybe even learn something. More dangerous
is the fear of what you can't see but intuit is somewhere close, ready to
pounce. What you can't see may still hurt you or, at the very least, cause you
to experience uncertainty and dread. The third fear is like an inner minefield that you traverse as you identify, accept, and process truths—such as
the inexorable advance of middle age and beyond. It's the realization that
we all have an expiration date, secret but certain.

That's life: the leopard you see; the one you don't see; and the one
that prowls stealthily through your dark places. The first leopard for me,
up to this point, is Parkinson's. I know its habits. I know its territory. I
know its cruelty. I know when it's safe to get out of the jeep, and when
it's not.

The second is the leopard I don't see. It's that gut feeling that something is wrong, very wrong. Something is out there waiting to pounce. No
warning, no negotiation, no accommodation. This foreboding is a recent
development, something that is common for many of us in middle age, and
which has intensified for me with the discovery and removal of the spinal
tumor.

And then, with my fall in the kitchen, a new existential crisis emerged.
This third fear is manifest in my Gollum-like scrambling along the length
of the tent. It's the unknown dangers that paralyze: Darkness. Confusion.
Solitude. Vulnerability. Essentially blindfolded, grasping for a familiar
shape, a handhold that is stable and can be trusted, but finding only the
temporary and unstable as I negotiate my way, pleading my case before
gravity. The stakes are high; not only could I damage myself, I could harm

others who share my space. I pray that I'll find my way, however unsure I may be of the path.

Sometimes the voices that guide me through my night-walking are interrupted by Tracy's soft whisper: "Honey, be careful."

"Good idea, sweetie. I'll try to be careful. Go back to sleep."

In that same "nothing to fear" speech, Franklin D. Roosevelt also said, "Only a foolish optimist can deny the dark realities of the moment."

I accept the optimist part, but now, I also admit to its foolishness.

20

FATHER TIME

I thought I had fear under control. Thoroughly contained. I had mitigated it with confidence and reason. But Africa reminded me that I'm full of shit.

ANTIGONISH
BY WILLIAM HUGHES MEARNS

Yesterday, upon the stair,
I met a man who wasn't there
He wasn't there again today
I wish, I wish he'd go away . . .

Parkinson's, for obvious reasons, is primarily thought of as a movement disorder; resting tremor, slowness, or bradykinesia. For us long-timers, walking and balance are a bitch. PD is also a *non-movement* disorder; changes in mood and sleep, fatigue, difficulty speaking, as well as digestive tract issues. When our behavior even hints at any of these changes, we first try to attribute them to aging, or more often, we just keep it to ourselves.

A Parkinsonian condition I rarely contemplated before now, much less spoke of, is cognitive change: loss of memory, confusion, delusions, and dementia. What am I thinking, and *how* am I thinking? What do others think I'm thinking? Am I thinking at all? Where are my car keys? Oh, yeah. I can't drive anymore.

You see what I'm saying. I'm sometimes frustrated by the effort it takes to recall simple words, like "respective," or "anagram," or the name of the new Giants quarterback (his name is "Jones").

Tracy and friends our age insist they experience similar lapses in memory and recall. But in my case, I worry that these brain delays could signal further progression of Parkinson's. I agree that we're all going through a bewildering age, and everyone fears dementia, but the fact is, cognitive decline is part of the disease profile, which creates a reasonable concern about eventual dementia.

Here is the kind of thing I'm talking about. I am standing in my New York office, in front of the television, shifting from foot to foot, golfer's stance, without swinging. I do this as a sensory exercise; careful to not lock up my knees, I keep my legs alive and active. The cable news program I'm watching goes to commercial. It's an ad for Nuplazid, a newly FDA-approved drug developed for Parkinson's patients. Our Foundation has a relationship with Acadia Pharmaceuticals, developers of this particular drug; a welcome therapeutic for an underserved aspect of the disease.

This drug targets Parkinson's psychosis, which often involves depression, paranoid thinking, and hallucinations; people and things that aren't there, a misunderstanding of events unfolding. The commercial opens on a handsome, dignified-looking man, an upscale home, a pastoral setting. He gazes into the distance with a placid expression. The dog at his side suddenly morphs into two dogs. The man looks to his wife, who approaches. Mysteriously, she is suddenly joined by another man. Our hero's expression changes to one of confusion and suspicion. It goes on from there, now showing him benefitting from the effects of Nuplazid, clear-eyed and helping his grandchild with a painting.

From the point of view of its target audience, it's a jarring piece of video. To see an ad for aspirin and know how a headache feels; or for Claritin (*Hey, I've got allergies, too*); or for any product that addresses your need and promises to fix you—makes you feel that someone's looking out for you. When you're a candidate for a shared experience with the model patient in the ad, and that shared experience is delusion and dementia, you snap to attention.

I don't know quite what to make of this commercial. "What did you think?" I say to the person on my left, who isn't there.

He is not a hallucination, or a delusion, or the man upon the stair in William Hughes Mearns's classic poem, but the side effect of a drug originally developed for geriatric flu. It was discovered anecdotally to provide relief from dyskinesias, the spastic head and body movements that are themselves the side effect of levodopa, still the gold standard in PD pharmaceutical therapy. I know this sensation of a peripheral presence is just a side effect of my meds. What's happening to the handsome man in the pastoral setting with the phantom dog, is not happening to me. I can relate to him, though; I've had as real an approximation to Parkinson's psychosis as you can get. The horrible hallucinations in Baltimore—the result of my anti-dyskinesia meds interacting with opiate anesthetic—gave me a window into what may await.

Talkin' About Degeneration

I just woke up, not yet showered. I'm sitting in my home office and watching an episode of *Alone*, on Hulu—a show where survivalists are left alone in the wild to fend for themselves until they go crazy. It's my new binge. Tracy stops into the room to remind me of plans we've made for this evening, which I have no recollection of. Just then, one of our adult daughters pokes her head into the doorway and asks me if I'd like a cup of coffee. I respond, "Yes. Thanks, Sky."

Her shoulders slump a little and she makes her *Oh, Dood,* face. "Nope, wrong one. I'm Aquinnah."

"Oops, my bad. I don't have my glasses on." Again, the face. Aquinnah has a state-of-the-art bullshit detector.

"It happens all the time," she says.

"Hey, it's a classic mistake. My mother did it, too. She'd go through all four of my siblings' names before she got to 'Mike.'" I turn to Tracy, looking for help, but her expression tells me none is on offer.

I attempt a pushback. "You know how it is, Tra. With your sisters. I'm sorry, you call Dana by the wrong name, sometimes."

And then, as if I'm hallucinating, I hear Dana's voice say, "Michael?"

Oh my god, did I channel her? After a brief moment of utter confusion, I realize that my sister-in-law's voice is coming from my iPhone. "Is that Dana?"

"Yes!" Tracy whispers. "What are you doing? It's six thirty in the morning. Hang up!"

But I didn't call Dana. I didn't touch my phone; it's on the coffee table. I reach for it, and speak. "Dana, is that you?"

"Yeah. Michael?"

"I apologize, I didn't mean to . . ."

"It's fine," she says through a yawn. "Butt dial?"

My butt was nowhere near the phone.

Tracy immediately gets it: "Mike, when you said 'Sorry' with your Canadian accent, it sounded like 'Siri.'"

"I have a Canadian accent?"

"Yes, you do."

"Oh. Then it's vestigial."

"Anyway, your phone heard 'Siri' and 'call Dana'—and it did."

Having overheard all of this, Dana cuts in. "Can I go back to bed now?"

Tracy, Aquinnah, and I reply as a chorus. "Yes."

"See you soon. Love to Mitch and the kids!" I add. I pocket my phone and look to my wife and daughter. "Can *I* go back to bed now?"

I can't spin more than one plate at a time these days. I have issues with executive function; I can't multitask. Whatever it looks like I'm doing, I'm really doing something else, perhaps unintentionally. Does that make me old, distracted, or in the grip of something more sinister?

My Two Dads

My father died in January 1990, when I was in my late twenties. Tracy and I were in our second year of marriage; Sam was six months old. Our photo albums contain only a few precious images of grandfather and grandson in the brief window of time they shared. We called his passing sudden, but Dad had been in poor health for years. Chronically overweight, he suffered from type 2 diabetes and heart disease. All this considered, we still hoped and expected he'd live beyond sixty-one years. I loved him, and still think about him every day.

Being a military man, it always agitated my father that I never learned to tie a tie. Getting dressed in my parents' home for his funeral, once again I struggled. Even on this day, I could not manage a simple knot for my dad. My frustration was tinged by a measure of shame; I just didn't know how to do it. My best attempt being my last, it still looked like a tourniquet. Stepping into the hallway, the first person I met, dressed and ready, was my father-in-law, Stephen. He and Tracy's mom, Corky, had flown to Vancouver for the service.

"Do you mean for your tie to look like that?" Stephen asked. "On purpose?"

"No, and it's a problem," I allowed, confessing my sartorial short-comings.

Stephen did a quick demo on his own tie, which I copied. After a few folds and follow-throughs, I produced a reasonable double Windsor. I tucked it into my suit jacket and patted it down. It looked good. For the first time since I was called home with the news about Dad, I managed a small smile.

"I'm not going to tell my dad you helped me out on this."

Stephen moved an imaginary zipper across his lips and turned a key.

That was Stephen—for thirty years, an ideal father-in-law. By profession, an attorney, financial advisor, and life coach, he'd guide clients not only to manage their finances, but to take a broader view of life's possibilities. A plaque on his desk read: "Professional Fear Remover." "Yes," he would encourage a young ad exec and his wife, "have another child. Get that bigger house. Go for that better job."

People often approached me with a look of recognition, and then . . . "Are you Stephen Pollan's son-in-law?"

Not surprised by the question, I'd nod. "Yes, I am."

What they'd say next, I'd heard so many times, I could mouth it along with them: "He changed my life." They'd recount how Stephen had helped them conquer some fear, improve their employment situation, or find new confidence to make big life choices. Risk and reward. Many would offer a name and a brief description of their experience with Stephen. "Tell him Debbie from Staten Island said hello. He helped us buy our condo five years ago."

I'd tell Stephen, and he would remember. "Oh, yes. Debbie. With the poodle."

In early 2018, Stephen had been living with cancer for a while, and he was beginning to fail, physically. There would be no further intervention. He had slowed down, but his spirit and sense of humor remained lively. Still funny, still wise, he seemed unconcerned about his own condition, beyond how it affected his family. I knew he was spending some time alone in the apartment; well, not completely alone: he and Corky had a miniature Himalayan cat, the size of a ground squirrel. Coco would scamper down his arm to steal sips from his water glass.

Once a week or so, I'd visit Stephen. I'd always bring along a brown bag and a good book for him. Lately, he favored novels by my friend Harlan Coben; he couldn't get enough of sports agent–turned–crime solver Myron Bolitar, Harlan's signature character. In the brown bag: chocolate éclairs.

One rainy Thursday morning in January, I let myself into the apartment and made my way to the kitchen, where I knew I'd find Stephen sitting at the table with a cup of coffee, perusing the *Times*, the same tableau as in his Connecticut kitchen. Greeting me with a smile, he rose with effort and collected the book, placing it on the table next to the paper. I gave him the bag. "Thanks," he said. "Maybe later. I'm not hungry right now."

A little rumpled, he looked paler than the sunburned, goateed Stephen from last summer, captaining his Vineyard porch deck overlooking Menemsha Sound. After all, it was now winter in Manhattan, and he had lost some weight, though he didn't seem noticeably gaunt. A little slower, a little quieter. Chatty, but in softer tones.

We sat at the table for a while and talked about family, the kids. Coco sipped Stephen's water, but had no interest in my Starbucks nonfat cappuccino. My meds were kicking in, and I was enjoying being in Stephen's company. Before long, I caved and ate one of his éclairs.

We moved into the TV room, turned on CNN, and grumbled about Trump for a while. Then the doorbell rang. I understood that I would be the one to get up and answer it, even though I was moving badly that day. After a moment's hesitation, I determined that it wasn't the front door, but the service door, all the way across the apartment, beyond the kitchen. I stumbled to the rear vestibule and squinted through the peephole in the center of the steel door. The lens probably hadn't been cleaned since 1967; I could make out no more than the hazy outline of a serial killer.

I checked around to make sure the cat wasn't underfoot, and then opened the door.

"I'm from Med Supply, delivering the hospice stuff," the man said.

"Oh, okay. Come in." I lurched back to the TV room, the guy following with a cart stacked with a shower chair, an oxygen pump, tanks, a breathing mask, and other paraphernalia. By the time we reached the den, Stephen was in the doorway.

"Delivery," I said.

Stephen surveyed the cart and its contents. "Oh, yeah. Right."

"Where does this stuff go?" the man inquired. Stephen pointed to the master bedroom.

Once inside the room, Mr. Hospice turned and began to explain each piece of equipment, how to set it up and how it was used. The more granular the detail, the blanker the expressions on both my and Stephen's faces. I stopped the guy mid-spiel, turned to Stephen, and asked, "Are you getting this?"

My father-in-law shrugged and made a face. "Are you?"

"Not really."

The guy looked us both over, then inquired, "Excuse me, which one of you is the patient?"

Stephen's lips broke into a sly smile. He rolled his eyes toward me and raised his eyebrows, ever so slightly; another subtle shrug. I was a little surprised at the question, although I admit I wasn't looking too "Marty McFly" in my sweatpants and old T-shirt, a few days' growth on my chin.

"Do you have the directions written down somewhere?" I asked the guy.

"Sure," he said. He handed me an info sheet and a receipt. I fumbled in my pocket for a tip. Accepting it, he said, "Good luck. I'll find my way to the door."

"Yeah, would you?" I said. "And mind the cat."

Once the guy was out of sight, Stephen turned to me, and incredibly, let loose a laugh. I managed to laugh, too.

Stephen passed three weeks later, with his family gathered around. His wife, Corky; Tracy and her siblings, Michael, Lori, and Dana; their spouses and all of our kids, surrounded the bed in a semicircle. I scanned the adoring faces in the room. Much sadness, but no despair. A letting go, unforced and natural.

I thought about the universality of this quiet ritual. *People have been doing this for tens of thousands of years, in caves, in deerskin tents, in castles, in hospital rooms.* This impulse for a communal, peaceful, and spiritual final observance is one of humanity's higher instincts.

In our family vigil, there was love for him and for each other, and a sincere aura of acceptance, which was a big part of Stephen's philosophy. The prevailing mood and spirit around Stephen—gratitude—was the very essence of the man. That's what he inspired in all of us. Always thankful for everything in his life, his gratitude was manifest in how much he loved his wife and family, and how appreciative he was for all of his experiences, positive and negative. A true optimist, he was known for his trademark assurance, "Just wait, kiddo, it gets better."

The core lesson Stephen left with me was this: With gratitude, optimism becomes sustainable.

21

ALL THINGS CONSIDERED

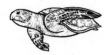

The loss of my father-in-law in January, a few weeks after the abrupt departure from our Turks and Caicos vacation, marked the beginning of 2018—my annus horribilis. As the events of the year tumbled on, culminating in the trip to Africa, Stephen's message of gratitude was overshadowed by the wall of my perceived miseries and resentments: the spine surgery, my broken arm, the isolation and melancholy during recovery, the TV binge-ing, the missed time with my family, the anger directed largely at myself. I recognized the value of Stephen's insights, but attempting to live his *It gets better* mantra was like trying to float a stone in water. It would drop and sink, the weight of my self-concern pulling me under along with it. Joyce, my Jungian analyst, advised, "Go with it. It's telling you something. Go deep. You can find truth in the depths."

And so I searched the deep, and found some treasure there. I realized that my gratitude, my optimism, had been hijacked by fear. My broken arm eventually pointed me toward an understanding, a prolonged epiphany that wasn't so much about my physical and mental travails, as it was about the fears they had created. Africa taught me about fear, in primal terms. I learned that there were things to be afraid of; things that went bump in the night. But in the months leading up to that trip, I had gotten lost in more conceptual fears: fear of my circumstances, fear of what the future could bring, and fear of my emotional reaction to it all.

There's a homily that suggests that "the opposite of fear is faith." Recalling the plaque on my father-in-law's desk—*Professional Fear Remover*—I consider the role gratitude played in his life. I'm beginning to see that faith, or fear's opposite, can be expressed as gratitude, which has always been the bedrock of my optimism.

I've spent sufficient time and energy dissecting what went wrong; I'm ready to reconnect with everything that went right.

Good Medicine

Something new happens today.

My neurologist, Dr. Susan Bressman, conducts my quarterly Parkinson's exam, a methodical set of skill, movement, and cognitive assessments. She tests my reflexes with a rubber mallet, and the assault on my patella produces a bouncy response; I kick out like a Rockette. After tapping my knees, she flips the rubber hammer and uses the other end as a scraping tool on the sole of my foot, checking the plantar reaction. My feet remain mostly numb, as do portions of my legs between the joints—hip to knee to ankle—so normally this poking and prodding doesn't bother me, no matter how aggressively she digs at my sole. But today, it hurts, which is the good news. "That's your spine," she says. "Less pressure on the cord, so it has finally started to ease up. It's getting better."

Getting better. Echoes of Stephen, but these are two words I've never heard from Sue. Her area of expertise is Parkinson's, a degenerative illness. While you won't die *from* Parkinson's, per se, you will die *with* it. Complications from the disease, such as the diminished ability to swallow, can lead to aspirating food or pneumonia, and these contributing factors can be lethal. Until we find a cure (and we will), "getting better" isn't part of the vernacular.

Sue's words of encouragement don't refer to Parkinson's, but to my recovery from the spine surgery. This is in line with Dr. Theodore's prognosis: eighteen to twenty-four months for my body to heal from the invasive trauma of the procedure, and for the spine to achieve a new standard for normal. I'm right on schedule.

I remind myself that this odyssey has not been about restoration, but about intervention; not a reset to zero, though maybe at least back to where I was before the tumor advanced and Dr. Theodore's knife caressed my spine. The damage done to my strength and mechanical function could not be erased, but I'm grateful that further deterioration was halted, and I'm no longer living with constant pain, or facing a future of almost certain paralysis. I'll take my victories where I find them, and today I feel, yes, *better*.

Pleased that this other health crisis is in abeyance, Sue shifts the discussion back to Parkinson's. Nina is with me for today's appointment. A keen listener and more likely than I am to retain details, she reports to Sue that she sees less foot-dragging and shuffling in recent months. Tracy, Nina, and Sue are the first witnesses to any change, large or small. I'm humbled by their efforts and caring attention. Purely by virtue of the fact that I'm the one actually living it, my knowledge of the disease is deeper than theirs, but not by much. Luckily for me, they know that I'm not the sum total of my symptoms.

It's a good visit and a positive assessment. All the boxes are checked: My current combination of PD meds seem to be working, my blood pressure is stable, and my sleeping has improved. Another key factor to this relative wellness is my continuing physical therapy sessions with Ryan. Now familiar with the regimen, I find moments at home, at work, and out in the world, to rotate my hips, knock off a quick set of ab contractions, or sneak in some calf stretches, while naming all of the Beatles' albums in order of release. I feel appropriately fit.

That doesn't mean I'm moving in any way resembling *normal*. I still fall once or twice a day, often more, but I've learned to fall more efficiently and less dangerously. I must simply accept this as part of my routine. I've also learned to accept the need to consult an inventory of options before I make a move. There's a drink on the table in front of me; I need to carry it across the room. Do I stand first, and then pick up the drink from the table? Or should I pick up the drink first? With my left hand? Is it stable? Which foot should I lead with? Depending on how I'm oriented, the left foot may be preferable, but if it fails in the process, my stride on the right will suffer. If I don't fall during this mission, I will, at the very least, spill the drink. This creates more choices: Should I take the direct route across the carpet, or do I stick to the room's perimeter, like a mouse? I'll go with the latter, so when I do spill, it's a quick wipe with a paper towel instead of a bill from the carpet cleaner. Or I could land on my face and break my nose.

Choices.

I have this conversation with myself thousands of times a day. One of me usually knows what he's talking about.

Hollywood Ending

2019 offers a reset, presenting opportunities to patch up a few still-tender wounds from the prior year. My agent, Nancy Gates, receives a call from Spike Lee's office. "Netflix is offering to fund a pick-up day on Spike's production, *See You Yesterday*," Nancy tells me. This is the film shoot I missed on that pivotal day in August, when I fell and broke my arm.

The first Saturday in February, I travel to location at a high school in the Bronx. The director, Stefon Bristol, greets me on the classroom set with joy and relief. Stefon is young and dynamic, and I can tell by the cast and crew's devotion that he knows exactly what he's doing. Gaffers, grips, production assistants, and the other actors introduce themselves, shake my hand with seeming reverence, or take a quick selfie. They're treating me like Jimmy Stewart. *Am I that old?*

Anyway, I love it. This is going to be fun.

I'm playing a high school science teacher. It's the final day of the school year, and I am chiding two of my best students (Eden Duncan-Smith and Danté Crichlow) on their joint senior presentation, wherein they assert the possibility of time travel. I give them a B+. In answer to their protestations, I insist, "If time travel were possible, it would be the greatest ethical and philosophical conundrum of the modern age." After the students exit, I mutter, "Time travel. Great Scott." Obviously, there is value in having me utter that line. Yeah, it's an inside joke, but it's a clever one, in a well-crafted script.

The film had officially wrapped production last fall, so it flattered and pleased me greatly that they would reassemble the cast and crew for one day, just to pick up this scene. As the resolution to my busted-arm-no-show, it is an ending right out of the movies.

Or better put in golf terms, it is a mulligan, a do-over, a breakfast ball.

What Happens in Vegas

I'm speaking—actually I'm shouting—into my iPhone at Tracy, as I navigate a raucous Las Vegas casino at happy hour.

"Sorry, honey. I'm taking a shortcut through the slot machines."

"To the blackjack tables?"

She knows me. "No, I'm meeting the guys for dinner. I may play later . . ."

"Okay, but if you play, promise me you'll win."

"I'll speak to management."

She laughs. "How was golf today? Did you play well?"

"How did I play?" I chortle. "Terrible. Bad. Really bad."

"*Really* bad?"

"The worst. I fell a couple of times, sliced some shots into the succulents. I lost about twenty quality golf balls."

Tracy pauses, confused. "Why are you so chipper?"

"Honey. I'm golfing again."

Every year, usually in February when there's no golf in the Northeast, George, Harlan, and I, and a fourth we pick up (last year it was my brother, Steve; this year it's Harlan's friend James Bradbeer, who answers to "Brad"), head to warmer climes to play a few rounds. Previous trips took us to Florida or Pebble Beach. Last year, in Los Angeles, was the last time I played, pre–back surgery. It was a debacle, and I haven't played since. Now, we're in Las Vegas.

My return to the links with the guys has special meaning—even though I didn't play well this morning, our first round of the trip. We picked a beautiful course, winding through craggy hills and mesas. Because it's so arid, there was very little grass on the fairway. Ideally, you want to hit the ball long—far enough to fly the scrabble and drop onto the green, or at least onto the fringe.

A few of the holes were too daunting, so I sat them out, distracting myself with the desert flora and fauna, clusters of cacti and winter flowers showing off. At the fifth hole, I spotted a coyote, slinking through the rocks that lined the cart path. Arriving at the seventh tee, I encountered a roadrunner. You can't make this stuff up. *Note to self: Watch for falling anvils.*

I hadn't been sure I'd make this trip, or that I would ever play golf again. But I'm here. I take the sighting of the roadrunner as a good omen, two holes ahead of the coyote. *Beep-beep.*

The next day, we are scheduled to play a mountain course regarded by the golfing press as a true test of skill. It's an hour's drive south of Las Vegas, and even though we have a noon tee time, we leave the hotel at 9:00 to allow for a stop on the way. Harlan has a friend who lives near Henderson, a gentleman that all three of us have an individual connection with: re-tired senator Harry Reid. Obviously, George knows the senator and has dealt with him many times, both as a political operative and as a journalist. Harlan first met him in 2001. A fan of his books, Reid, along with former senator Tom Daschle, invited Harlan to Capitol Hill to talk crime novels and politics.

It was the beginning of a lasting friendship.

My first contact with the senator came in the summer of 2006, when his office reached out to me during my summer vacation on Martha's Vine-yard. Senator Reid came on the line to solicit my involvement in backing congressional midterm candidates who were pro–stem cell research. I felt privileged to be in a position to make a difference. I hit the campaign trail that fall, and agreed to a media blitz. Amazingly, all of the candidates we supported during that midterm election won their seats, ushering in seven years for Harry Reid as majority leader, and renewed enthusiasm in Wash-ington for scientific freedom and advancements in research. We did some good work, and I'm proud of it.

This morning's side trip is a bonus. Mr. Reid is a gracious host and a gifted raconteur; listening to his stories, we almost lose track of time. Har-lan glances at his watch, and announces that we have to go if we're going to make our tee time. We thank the senator, pile back in the car, and hurry to the course.

In spite of yesterday's mediocre play, I feel encouraged and excited. Maybe I'll get lucky on some challenging shots. It's a gorgeous morning in the high desert, but chilly, in the low 50s, about ten degrees cooler than the previous day. I have a few stumbles, no serious falls, and I am able to execute full swings, albeit with varying results.

Satisfied with the holes we've played, and feeling a chill we aren't dressed for, we decide to head in for lunch after one last hole. Both George and Brad launch decent shots on either side of the fairway. Harlan addresses the ball and spanks it straight down the middle, a typical Coben golf shot. I'm the last to go, as usual, but something tells me this shot will be momentous. This ball's got eyes. It knows where to go. And sure enough, my swing is pure. The ball explodes from my clubhead and rockets down the center of the fairway, flying over Harlan's ball by a good five yards. It's the shot of my life.

As I walk past Harlan's ball, I point to it and say, "Nice shot." And in the parlance of the game, "Harlan, you're away."

"No fair," he says. "You have a titanium arm."

We enjoy lunch in the clubhouse, talk golf and politics, and review life's rich pageant. All the while, something remarkable is happening outside: It's snowing. We comment on the irony that we left the Northeast to go to the desert Southwest, where big, chunky flakes are currently drifting from the sky. Soon the entire course is blanketed in pure, cleansing snow; the morning's magic is sealed and sanctified. Apparently, the snow extends all the way to the Vegas strip, which could use some sanctifying.

———

I double bogeyed that final hole of the morning, even with the towering tee shot. It wasn't a *Rocky* moment; I can't putt worth a damn. But it doesn't matter—the day held more important meaning.

In the months since our golf trip, I haven't played much. The progress of my game has been mitigated by my physical regression. I'm at peace with that. Golf gifted me almost twenty years of abundant memories. The friendships remain, which is the best takeaway.

I gave golf a shot. It was a hell of a shot. I'm away.

Exit Laughing

Whither my golf game? Whither the second act of my career?

The trip to Vegas was reward enough for the years I'd put into the game—or should I say, the years the game put into me. But the same can't quite be said for the final phase of my show biz career.

The Good Wife had spoiled me with its great writing, genius cast, and the opportunity to inhabit a multifaceted character without the onus of being number one on the call sheet. The producers were willing to accept my limitations, while astutely exploiting my strengths. Somehow, I made the calculation that if I could do that many guest shots and consistently perform well, maybe I was ready to do a series again.

The rest is sort of a blur. Several years ago, upon mentioning to my agents that I might be up for headlining a show, they immediately put me together with two young writers, both eager and thrilled to be working with me. Emboldened by the positive reaction to my role on *Curb*, we decided not to shy away from PD and pitched a show based on the experiences recounted in my first two books: basically, a dad with Parkinson's. We called it *The Michael J. Fox Show* (*Seinfeld* was already taken).

Having heard nothing more than the concept and a few personal anecdotes, every network offered to buy the show during the pitch meeting. That's not normal. Caught up in the incredible velocity of the process, I found myself committed to twenty-two episodes at NBC. The deal was made without the inclusion of my partner, Nelle. It was my grievous mistake in not making sure I had someone who was looking out for my interests, specifically. I didn't have the energy or the time, given my responsibilities as lead actor of the show, to execute the oversight that someone with an eponymous television series should be prepared to deliver.

We shot a good pilot; Betsy Brandt, Wendell Pierce, and the rest of the cast were hugely talented. But very quickly, there was trepidation on the part of the network, as if the execs suddenly awoke, slapped their collective foreheads, and gasped, "Oh, he really does have Parkinson's." I sensed them observe me tremoring during rehearsal and whispering to their colleagues, "What's wrong with him?" I think Parkinson's freaked them out, which was problematic, because it was the premise of the show.

The first season was also the last. Ultimately, I didn't have the focus or the bandwidth to administer the life support the show would need to make it. That's on me, and I'm fine with that. As I've said before, I can play anyone as long as they have Parkinson's; this is especially true when I'm playing a version of myself.

As if I'd never gone away, *The Good Wife* has me back for a few episodes during their final season. It is a tonic. Over the next couple of years, I accept two guest shots on other network shows that are not as satisfying. These are the last acting roles I've done, and most likely the last I will do. I feel no sadness in making this prediction. Like Tracy said after we sold our house in the country, the one the kids had grown up in: "This house owes us nothing." I feel the same way about my second act, and golf, too, for that matter. They owe me nothing. They both took me further than I expected, to places I may never visit again.

There is a variable that hadn't been present in the *Scrubs* to *Rescue Me* to *The Good Wife* run. In those shows, I had figured out a way to incorporate my extraneous movement, my spasticity, even my rigidity. I didn't have to move much to play any of those characters. A chair, a cane, a desk to lean on; I could get around the set without calling attention to my limitations.

But not being able to *speak* reliably is a game-breaker for an actor. Difficulty in forming words is one problem; the other is remembering the words I am meant to say. Previously in my career, I had no problem with line memorization. In fact, as I've said about the days of *Family Ties*, I enjoyed a near-photographic memory. But recently that changed. It's a different story on these last two dramas, in which I play lawyers. "Legalese" is difficult to learn and speak, never mind understanding what the hell I'm saying.

First, I agree to a five-episode arc in *Designated Survivor*, playing a white-shoe Washington, D.C., attorney, representing the cabinet as they try to remove the president of the United States via the twenty-fifth amendment. For me, "survivor" is the key word. While this role is challenging, and fun creatively, it is a self-inflicted assault on my brain and body. Not only do I endure a perfect storm of symptoms, but I have to film during February and March in Toronto; snow and ice, and long distances to walk between sets in the enormous warehouse studio. I don't know it yet, but I am a little more than a month away from surgery on my spine.

In the complicated plot, my character is both ally and adversary of the president, played by Kiefer Sutherland, an old friend of mine. We worked together in the '80s on *Bright Lights, Big City*. A terrific guy, at once folksy and urbane, Kiefer welcomes me on the set, a happy reunion. As I'd remembered, Kiefer likes to work fast, briskly, picking up on other actors' cues, with very little air between the lines. Although I enjoy this quick and snappy style, I just can't oblige. "Whereas in the party of the second part . . ." leads immediately into "habeas corpus . . ."and then right into "posse comitatus . . ." I'm lost, and have to start again. I cannot get through a scene without having to stop, and with confusion and embarrassment, call out to the script supervisor: "Line, please."

I had enjoyed this formal lexicon in the past; I nailed it on *Boston Legal* and *The Good Wife*. I loved the musicality of it, and I had no problem in rolling out the legalese. But this is different. I know the editor will save my ass, and he does. But it has not been a pleasant experience. I no longer have the facility, and the thrill is gone.

On *The Good Fight*, a spin-off of *The Good Wife*, I am Louis Canning again, so that familiarity is helpful. But in the few years since I last embodied the character, much has changed with the show, and with me. The production is leaner and on a tighter budget, with a shorter production schedule and more scenes to film in a day. They can't allow me the rest and recuperation between scenes and film days that had been afforded by the larger mother show. The upshot is that I play three six-page scenes in the course of a day, covered in such a way that I have to perform all three

scenes at once, eighteen pages at a time, instead of shooting the scenes in-
dividually.

It crushes me.

One more reference to Tarantino's *Once Upon a Time . . . in Hollywood*: Leonardo DiCaprio, playing a cowboy actor who's seen better days,
keeps screwing up his lines while doing a guest shot on a popular TV
Western. Furious at himself over his chronic inability to remember and
deliver the dialogue (we've seen him going over and over the script in
scenes prior), he retreats to his boxy dressing room trailer, takes a stance
in front of the mirror, and berates himself viciously over his abject failure.

I feel his pain. I've obviously been there. But weighed against everything
else in my life, I don't find it worthy of self-excoriation. I'm not sure it ever
did, but especially now, my work as an actor does not define me. The na-
scent diminishment in my ability to download words and repeat them verba-
tim is just the latest ripple in the pond. There are reasons for my lapses in
memorization—be they age, cognitive issues with the disease, distraction
from the constant sensations of Parkinson's, or lack of sensation because
of the spine—but I read it as a simple message, an indicator. There is a
time for everything, and my time of putting in a twelve-hour workday,
and memorizing seven pages of dialogue, is best behind me. At least for
now. In fairness to myself and to producers, directors, editors, and poor
beleaguered script supervisors, not to mention actors who enjoy a little
pace, I enter a second retirement. That could change, because everything
changes. But if this is the end of my acting career, so be it.

Tattoo You

I got a tattoo in SoHo from an artist with the sobriquet "Mr. K." It's a fine-
lined black-and-gray sea turtle, gliding palmward along the inside of my
right forearm. I posted a picture of it on Instagram, straight from the par-

lor chair. The typical reaction from followers was: "*You* got a tattoo? Who gets their first tattoo at fifty-eight?"

Good question. I have an answer: That would be me. Given the prevailing cultural norm—everybody is inked these days—I considered the *absence* of a tattoo on my body as a commensurate act of rebellion. This badge of ink doesn't exactly make me the Illustrated Man, and Tracy says if I get one more of these things, she'll kill me. So why now? It all leads back to the turtle.

It was New Year's 1999, the eve of the new millennium. Our family was on vacation in the Virgin Islands. Tracy and I were alone at the beach at the end of the day, and I was distracted. I was struggling to decide whether to continue with another season of *Spin City*, or retire and create a research-based Parkinson's foundation. I waded into the ocean for the year's last swim. Snorkeling aimlessly through the grassy edge of the reef, I suddenly found myself beside a large and battered sea turtle. Something had taken a chunk out of his right front fin, and a nasty scar marked his beak. We swam together for a while. This guy had obviously been through a lot, and had earned the right to go where he wanted. He imbued me with a measure of his will. Sure, it might be easier to just flow with the current, but sometimes you have to risk charting a new course.

Two decades later, as I deliberated how best to go forward from the emotional and physical battering I'd been through, I thought of that stoic turtle. Getting tatted was a permanent gesture of respect and appreciation. In the same way I had used the X-ray of my arm to illustrate what had happened to me, the turtle tattoo made the invisible visible; it created a visual record of the power of resiliency, and the will to survive.

My turtle swims through five rings, ripples of water representing the five decades of my life. The rings also signify emergence, both his and mine. I've come through a difficult period, and now I swim in calmer waters. I have battle scars, and a tattoo to show for it.

22

SHAKE IT OFF

Every November in New York City, The Fox Foundation hosts a big gala. An enthusiastic crowd gathers to hear great musicians like the Who, Elvis Costello, Chris Martin, James Taylor, Paul Simon, John Mayer, Sheryl Crow, Dave Matthews, John Fogerty, Joan Jett, Bon Jovi, and Brad Paisley. We call the night "A Funny Thing Happened on the Way to Cure Parkinson's," so naturally we include comedians—Denis Leary, Ricky Gervais, David Letterman, Jon Stewart, Chris Rock, Jim Gaffigan, Amy Schumer, Robin Williams, John Mulaney, Colin Quinn, Tina Fey, and a rogue's gallery of others.

The guests are laughing, happy, and well fed. It's a pricey ticket, so we raise a lot of money, about $5 million in a night, all of which goes to research (the event is underwritten by our Board of Directors). Once we have you there, we stay out of your wallet; no auctions or further calls to contribute. It's a party to celebrate the year's progress, and a meet-and-mingle with supporters of our cause in the Parkinson's community.

Each year at the benefit, we impart the Foundation's mission and methods in the form of a short film. This is always coproduced by Nelle and me, with Nelle also contributing her considerable talents as director, a duty which she handles deftly, and with empathy and insight.

This year's film tells the story of Jimmy Choi, a Parkinson's patient and technology executive from Bolingbrook, Illinois. To say he's an activist and a fundraiser would sell him short; he's a part-time ninja for Parkinson's. His experience with the disease is personal, and to many PD patients, including and especially me, particularly powerful. As Jimmy opens up during his interview with Nelle and me, much of what he describes sounds familiar. Like I used to say when I was a kid, "It takes one to know one."

"I was diagnosed with young-onset Parkinson's in 2003, at the age of twenty-seven," Jimmy begins. "I didn't tell anyone I had PD for a while, not even my wife. For the next seven years, I ignored Parkinson's. I gained seventy pounds, which didn't help my deteriorating health. I needed a cane to walk. Clearly, I had just given up."

Echoes of my past demons: I was diagnosed with young-onset Parkinson's at the same stage of life, in my late twenties. Although I shared the news with Tracy, I kept it from most.

Jimmy continues. "Then I had two 'aha' moments. The first: Eight years into my disease, I was going down the stairs, carrying my nine-month-old son, Mason. I thought, *I don't need my cane—I've got the railing.* My son was tucked under my arm. One of my legs didn't move with me; in my mind I thought it was moving, but my leg stayed behind as I approached the second or third step. I fell the entire length of the staircase. Fortunately, I was able to keep Mason above me and he was not injured, but it was startling, to say the least. My home had been my 'safe zone,' the place where I could let my symptoms be free. I had the false sense that nothing bad could happen inside my house, buffered by the only people who knew I had Parkinson's."

This is so eerily close to my experience. Disastrous falls; the challenge presented by everyday routines. Similarly, I felt a false sense of security, more like hubris, in the privacy of my home. Until I snapped my arm. Now I can't walk into my own kitchen without having flashbacks. He probably feels the same way when he travels those stairs.

"The worst part wasn't hitting the ground; it was looking up at my wife and daughter. I'll never forget the expression of horror on their faces. It made me think, 'What have I reduced myself to at this moment? I've become a burden, a safety hazard. Just holding my son, I put both of us in danger.'"

This part of Jimmy's story reminds me of my last hangover; the look on Tracy's face—in her case, boredom—that caused me to stop drinking and face life with PD and a family. Another kind of awakening.

"It struck me right then—I had to change," Jimmy states. "I didn't like the way I was living. I had no idea what to do about it, but if I continued on this way, it wouldn't be good."

It's spooky to hear him say this. I had this moment, too, and it was powerful and revelatory.

"I began losing the weight, eating better, and taking walks with my family, but I wasn't *pushing* myself physically. Then I read about a Parkinson's patient who had finished a marathon, and it really inspired me. Before my diagnosis, I had been an athlete—captain of my high school football team, a wrestler, and a golfer. I decided to enter a 5K. Then I ran a 10K, and soon, a half-marathon. I was hooked. I couldn't believe how much better I felt with regular, rigorous exercise. I was able to get rid of the cane."

That's right, I thought; *just do the next right thing. Your family will see you stand up, step forward, and carry on.*

"I set a goal to train for the 2012 Chicago Marathon, only a few months away. Unfortunately, the race was closed; there was no way to register."

But there was. The Fox Foundation, like other charities, is granted a limited number of bibs in marathons and other big races, for runners to raise money for our cause.

"This was the first time I'd been in touch with the Foundation, since I avoided dealing with my Parkinson's for so long. Soon I was talking to Stephanie at Team Fox—she had one entry bib left for the Chicago Marathon. I've always thought that bib was meant for me.

"I ran the marathon for Team Fox, and this was my second '*aha*' moment. Not only did it connect me with the Foundation, which is now such a big part of my life, but it also gave me the impetus to 'come out' to my friends and family. I had to explain why I was raising money for Parkinson's research. I was blown away by their reaction. My friends and family listened to my story, and they were really there for me."

It's harder for a guy like Jimmy to reveal his diagnosis than it was for me— and it was definitely hard for me, so I can just imagine how it was for him. It's a very personal choice, very scary to "go public." That first expression of support from family and friends means everything.

"In only a month's time, I raised $5,000. After years of hiding, I opened up about my story and educated others about the disease. I did all of that in four weeks, versus the previous eight years when I did *nothing*. It was the most positive I'd felt in all the years since I was diagnosed. The Fox Foundation did that for me."

Jimmy's wife, Cherryl, adds, "Something clicked. Just signing up to be a part of something, to raise money for research, suddenly made it so much easier for us to talk to our friends and family. 'Jimmy has Parkinson's,' we finally told them. 'We're dealing with it.' It didn't feel so scary anymore."

Jimmy is smiling. "I went to my first Fox Foundation gathering not long after the Chicago Marathon. It was the Team Fox MVP Dinner in New York City, to celebrate top fundraisers. I sat down at a table with a group of strangers, other PD patients who have been my friends ever since. Suddenly, I realized there were people out there just like me, *living* with Parkinson's. Everybody had little bits of information and advice that I could use to make myself better, that I could learn from. And soon I knew enough to return the favor to others.

"The whole sense of a Parkinson's community suddenly came into play. The number of people we met at that first Fox event really jolted us. So many amazing patients and their families. We were inspired and excited by everyone on the staff of your Foundation. Cherryl and I knew then, 'We've got to do more. These people are busting their tails to find a cure for Parkinson's. We need to do more, because this is who I am now.'"

Patients like Jimmy take away the stigma: the common belief that Parkinson's is an old person's disease, that young people don't have it. Before we launched the Foundation, the young-onset community had not exercised its full potential to dynamically increase awareness, advocate politically, and raise money. The Foundation gave voice to their message: PD is here, it's real, and it can affect you or someone you know.

"I've now finished sixteen marathons for Team Fox, and over one hundred half-marathons. The event Cherryl and I started in Illinois, The Shake It Off 5K, has raised nearly $400,000. My body is strong. I still have symptoms and bad days, but I'm managing Parkinson's better than ever. On my daughter's urging, I trained and auditioned for *American Ninja Warrior*, her favorite show. I'm glad I did.

"I've competed on *Ninja Warrior* four times, now, and it's been a blast.

"I remember you once saying that the best expert on this disease is 'the patient.' A few years ago, I agreed to join The Fox Foundation's Patient Council, with thirty-four other patients from around the country, at different ages and stages of their disease. The folks at the Foundation truly want to know what is important to us—our daily challenges, and what the Foundation can do to help us improve our lives now.

"I also use the Foundation's online tool, Fox Trial Finder, to match me up with available clinical trials. More trials mean more shots on goal."

I appreciate the hockey metaphor. It's an apt one, because that's what we're about. Firing at this thing from every direction: slap shots, wrist shots, long shots; it's all about getting the puck across the line. We are relentless, and Jimmy embodies our patient-centric drive to succeed and find a cure.

"I know I have to live with this disease for many years to come, and I have to do my best to take care of myself. I want to be strong for my daughter and son. I want them to know that I'm trying my best. If they ever get into a position in life where they're faced with some hardship, they can think, 'What would my dad do?'"

I obviously relate to this desire. The mistake I make at times is to assume that my kids are looking at what I can't do, and not at what I can do. They see through the disease, and they see their dad.

"Everybody I've met through Team Fox—the patients, families, and Foundation staff—has a mindset to beat Parkinson's. I've surrounded myself with a positive circle of people, there to support me. No matter which way I fall, they're going to push me back up. That's been a huge key to where I am now."

Later, I tell Jimmy how touched I am by his testimonial. With a lump in my throat, I share with him: "You've pushed me back up a few times, brother. You don't even know it. There have been times I've thought of you, all that you've achieved, all you've given back to the Foundation, and it's helped me get through something. I've had a lot of mentors in my life, but I don't have many heroes. You're one of them."

A Solid Foundation

Our film about Jimmy Choi is one of the highlights of our gala event. The crowd is already attentive, responsive, and enthusiastic, and Jimmy's energy kicks it up to another level. Steve Winwood plays. The music is great, and the comics are hilarious. At some point after dinner, Tracy and I come onstage, stand at the podium, and thank people. I always have a headful of things I want to say, and Tracy, although sometimes shy at a microphone, is not averse to going off script and getting a laugh at my expense. If she leaves me an opening, I return the favor, à la Sonny and Cher (with less sequins and fringe). We go back and forth for a minute or two, and then realize we have business to attend to and return to our script on the teleprompter.

I am scanning a thousand faces in the ballroom, and thinking, *Look at what we did*. Nelle, Debi Brooks, and I, squatting in our former *Spin City* offices twenty years ago, laying out the blueprint for the Foundation, had no idea it would grow to this extent. I don't often get this kind of perspective.

Back in 2000, when we announced our first round of scientific grants, brain research was promising but significantly underfunded. We leapt in with full enthusiasm. Many people in this room have shown tremendous commitment since the Foundation's inception: board members and their associates, beyond generous in their support; our talented staff, led by Debi, Todd Sherer, and Sohini Chowdhury, and the dedicated scientists who are working every day to unlock this disease. There are patients with their families here tonight, too, and many are actual participants in our process— signing up for clinical trials; serving on our councils and committees; engaging in advocacy and community outreach; and fundraising through Team Fox, the special arm of the Foundation highlighted in the evening's film. Our staff in New York helps to guide and support these community fundraisers—6,400 separate events, and counting, worldwide. It's a badge of honor around our office, or at any of our meetings or conferences, to be identified as a Team Fox member. This group of volunteers have raised nearly $100 million for The Michael J. Fox Foundation, greatly contributing to our overall success.

It's incredible that in less than two decades, The Fox Foundation has funded $1 billion in research. One billion dollars is a lot of money, and twenty years seems like a long time, but in research terms, we're high-velocity. In the quest to cure Parkinson's, we're absolutely certain we are the tip of the spear.

I'm looking out at the sea of faces again. It strikes me that whenever I'm beating myself up over a personal setback, or feeling ineffective in my life, I need to reflect on this moment—this panoramic view in front of me—which is the result of an instinct to help, to embrace a community, and to try to make a difference. *Good things can come from bad things.*

Suddenly, the gala audience laughs. I snap out of my reverie and realize that Tracy just said something funny, and I missed it. I'm sure she'll be happy to repeat it on the car ride home.

Touch of Gray

The sentinel crow atop the highest bough of our old cedar tree emits a series of sharp caws that sends the songbirds, starlings, and sparrows bursting out of the surrounding treetops, flitting and flapping in retreat. It's not the crow that they're afraid of; it's what the crow is afraid of that has them in a panic. A hawk is tracing lazy circles in the sky above our neighborhood. The bird logic must be: *If we all move at once, there is safety in numbers.*

I'm observing this from my back porch. A pair of binoculars are close at hand, a Father's Day gift from my kids. I'm about to reach for them when Gus comes out to the porch. I glance at him in acknowledgment and watch as he does his own slow, hawklike circle. Once he's ready, he lowers himself, gingerly, to a sitting position beside me. I recognize the geriatric caution that goes into this effort, hovering over the landing zone. The last foot and a half of butt-drop, all gravity and luck.

"I'm watching the birds," I tell him. After a beat, he looks at me and takes in the yard as if he understands what I'm talking about. Maybe not. I hear the high *pip* sound of the hawk, which spooks a bunny out of the hedgerow. Gus lets go a low *woof* and initiates a "getting up" motion.

I laugh and he stops. "You're not chasing that rabbit. You're an old man." He *is* an old man. Let's face it: He is physiologically older than I am. He seems to have lost muscle mass in his hindquarters. His back legs don't serve him as well as they once did, getting in and out of cars, negotiating obstacles, running, and chasing rabbits. He has some tenderness in his hips, and his gait is compromised. He is slower, and can be a little mopey. He's a big dog, so it's obvious to us when he's lost weight. One hundred fifteen pounds in his prime, he's a little less than that now. We have to make an extra effort to keep him north of the one-hundred mark.

Cognitively, he's still solid. He impresses me as having a logical, intuitive, maybe instinctive understanding of sequencing: water-walk-food; who's coming home next; how soon will they be here; and what car will they be driving (he knows which one is mine). He grasps the concept of cause, effect, and consequence. Does that mean he understands past, present, and future? I think a dog is living all three at once. I've tried that; it doesn't work.

Parkinson's has taken away my sense of smell, but I'm told by my disgruntled family that Gus is a little more aromatic these days. We'll be watching TV, and suddenly noses crinkle and everyone clears out. I look to make sure Gus is actually in the room, so I know for sure it wasn't me.

Beyond all this *Old Yeller* boy-and-his-dog stuff, there are some real parallels. I see Gus getting older, grayer, shaggier, thinner. I'm pretty much the same, although I wish I had his waist.

Gus is twelve. Shouldn't be old for a dog, but it is, thus providing the rationale behind that faux formula of "seven human years to one dog year," probably manufactured to make us feel better about the brevity of a dog's lifespan. Given Gus's size and his genetic mélange of breeds, he's not expected to live much past fourteen. The way I see it, though, that's negotiable. Whatever the threat, I can attempt to forestall. There are effective meds for everything that ails a canine. If Gus needs an operation, he has a great vet. If a time comes when he can't use his hind legs, I'll have rear wheels made for him; a cart he can propel with his front paws.

Gus puts aging, and ultimately mortality, into perspective for me. I've availed myself of each of these options in my medical history: the standard cocktail of PD meds, surgery on my back and on my arm, and the use of a wheelchair. All to extend life and hopefully make the remainder of the ride as comfortable as possible.

I read somewhere that there is a red sea urchin, native to the South Pacific, that has been documented to live upward of 250 years. A freaking sea urchin. That spiny prick gets to hang out in the ocean for 250 years, and my dog, Gus, gets a dozen or so to roam the earth. Who do I see about that?

23

MIDNIGHT IN THE GARDEN

"Do you smell pot?" Tracy's asking over the music.

"Do I smell what? Pot? Do you?"

An exaggerated nod.

We're at Madison Square Garden. The band Vampire Weekend has sold out the house, which is impressive for a quirky, up-tempo jam band that once toured with the Bernie Sanders campaign.

"Nope, I can't smell it." I laugh, point at my nose, and make a shaky hand sign.

For some Parkinson's patients, the smell deficit is total, but for me, I can still pick up a faint trace of scent. Walk me blindfolded into a horse barn, and I can download enough olfactory info to prompt a "Where's the pony?" But tonight, *nada*, I can't whiff the weed. No question this sensory deprivation is a loss, but it may even predate my diagnosis, so it's been absorbed into normalcy. My sense of taste is also affected, but strangely, not my appetite, which accounts for my dad bod.

In the context of all the losses I've experienced in my twenty-nine years of living with the disease, these symptoms are the least of my problems. Still, for a fifty-eight-year-old man at a rock concert, if only for nostalgia's sake, the perfume of ganja would be nice. I don't smoke, myself, but who knows, maybe I'll catch a contact buzz while I wait for my own non-psychotropic drugs to kick in (Parkinson's meds, entirely buzz-less). Tracy, having easily decoded my hand signals, taps the tip of her own nose and smiles. "Too bad."

The band is killing it; with a world-class guitarist, two drummers, and a wickedly deft bass player, their beat is complex and infectious. On my left, two of our three daughters, Schuyler and Esmé, are swaying to the music. Sam is in Los Angeles, and Aquinnah is working (the world of advertising never rests). To my right, Tracy is, by now, flat-out grooving, soaking the music into her pores and letting it out with paroxysms of hip-swinging, arm-waving, and ass-shaking. The girl can dance.

Me, not so much. My dancing has never been good and my best moves are unintentional. Tracy dances at every concert we attend, and this factored into my decision to be here tonight. It takes an effort to make it out to a big public event, having nothing to do with being famous or recognized, but more with simple logistics. A regular at Madison Square Garden for years, I've been here for big fights, Rangers and Knicks games, and dozens of concerts. We've seen the Rolling Stones, U2, Pearl Jam, Springsteen, and one Friday night, my daughters even got me here to see Katy Perry. I know most of the security staff by sight and many by name, and they spoil me whenever I show up. Since I can't safely navigate my way through the throngs of concertgoers, nor travel the length of the world's most famous arena on foot, they provide me with a wheelchair and I spin through the bowels of the building, powered by an MSG escort.

I find that I'm actually okay with using a wheelchair now. I see it not as a tyrant, but as a tool. I've managed to live my life without Parkinson's defining me, so I'm no longer troubled by a simple chair with wheels. FDR would not allow himself to be photographed in a wheelchair. Neither would JFK. But I'm over it. I'm not the president of anything. I don't have to worry about Hitler or Castro assessing my vulnerabilities and weaknesses. I'm just a retired actor who wants to go to a concert with his wife and daughters. Roll on.

The MSG attendant, whose pushing etiquette is impeccable, stays beside Tracy and the girls at their pace, occasionally lobbing in a little New York Rangers gossip. He delivers us to our section. I rise from the chair, to no one's surprise or dismay. A few careful steps up a metal stairway and I plant my ass in my seat, mission accomplished. I've come to accept that *I take a village*. I'm part of the village, too; I contribute in every way I can, and try to be a solid citizen. I feel fortunate to be here, in this place, with these people that I love. The effort is 100 percent worth it—the music, the girls, the hint of pot smoke, and of course, Tracy.

Between songs, Esmé and Schuyler slip out of their seats and soon return with Vampire Weekend bucket hats. They look ridiculous, and beautiful. Tracy gives a thumbs-up to the hats, never once breaking her rhythm. On her feet the whole night, she's sublimely in sync with the pulse of the concert, and seems more like my girlfriend of three weeks than my wife of thirty-one years.

The young crowd sings along with the band and the whole joint is rocking. I may not be dancing but I'm standing, at times white-knuckling the handrail, and I'm singing along. I'm a worse singer than I am a dancer, but fortunately my sonic dissonance is subsumed by the amplified roar from the stage, from the far reaches of the building, and from the groundlings on the arena floor. The band slides into the opening chords of their current hit, "Harmony Hall." I join in on the chorus with its signature lyric: *I don't wanna live like this . . . but I don't wanna die.* God, tell me about it.

I carry that line in my mind now. I hear it in the car on SiriusXM radio, and I still puzzle over its resonance. The question is, which part of the dialectical pronouncement carries the most weight: *I don't wanna live like this* or *I don't wanna die?* Of course, I'm not taking into account lead Vampire

Ezra Koenig's meaning, motive, or method, nor his intention in creating the song in the first place, and I'm not going to him for the answer. I'm reminded of the time I played "Me and Julio Down by the Schoolyard" with Paul Simon at The Fox Foundation's annual fundraiser. During rehearsal, I hesitated over a lyric. I said to Paul, "It's so cryptic." He looked at me straight-faced and said, "Yes, Michael. Yes, it is." Poets and artists will always answer your questions about meaning with one of their own: *Well, what does it mean to you?* Don't count on them to stick around for your reply.

The truth is, I don't *want* to live like this, but I have found a way to accept the fact that I do. For every perilous trip across a room, when my meds are off and my steps are halting and erratic, there are also times when it all slips away. In those moments, like this night out with my family, I feel joy and contentment. In those moments, I have everything I need.

I had been experiencing a temporal compression, attempting to live the past, present, and future all at the same time. The lines were blurred.

When I visit the past now, it is for wisdom and experience, not for regret or shame. I don't attempt to erase it, only to accept it. Whatever my physical circumstances are today, I will deal with them and remain present. If I fall, I will rise up. As for the future, I haven't been there yet. I only know that I have one. Until I don't. The last thing we run out of is the future.

Really, it comes down to gratitude. I am grateful for all of it—every bad break, every wrong turn, and the unexpected losses—because they're real. It puts into sharp relief the joy, the accomplishments, the overwhelming love of my family. I *can* be both a realist and an optimist.

Lemonade, anyone?

Epilogue

A not-so-funny thing happened on the way to finishing this book. In the midst of personal introspection—so hyper-focused as to require a dental mirror—the world exploded, or rather imploded. Actually, both. After more than a year spent examining my life from an eyeball-to-navel perspective, my worldview was suddenly supersized, looking downward from thirty thousand feet at a planet in crisis. The travails and triumphs of one man suddenly seemed insignificant among the struggles of seven billion people, living and dying through a global pandemic.

Countries around the globe went into lockdown. We went inside and shut our doors, seeking refuge in quarantine. Yet somehow, existing separate and apart, we all had a shared experience.

I never thought of it this way, but for years I've been practicing my own version of social distancing—in my case, the length of an arm plus a cane between myself and others, as a means to protect people from the dangers of *me*. Frankly, I also kept an emotional distance, as in: *You can't relate to my problems.* Now I had company in my socially distanced isolation. Everyone kept a safe distance, concerned about their health and that of friends and family. Whatever our previous issues were, we all now shared the same big problem, and none of us knew what would happen next.

Shortly after New York City shuttered its businesses, restaurants, and bars, and limited the access to services, Tracy and I gathered our four children, three of whom were living on their own, and relocated to our summer home on Long Island. We sheltered in place. The six of us had not lived this closely together for years. In many ways, it was an experience I will never forget.

I was thankful to have my family safe and together, and we all found corners of the house in which to work or attend school remotely. We relished our nonwork hours to focus on each other, to assemble jigsaw puzzles, and watch old movies. Tracy cooked amazing meals, and we lingered around the dinner table, discussing the world and debating politics and social policies.

We were aware of the dichotomy of this situation. People infected with the virus were dying alone in hospitals, without the care and comfort of their family at their sides. At the same time, the virus brought families like ours closer to one another, huddled together inside. We were more connected to each other than ever before. Still, there were personal losses and disappointments.

My daughter Esmé graduated from high school in June, but like most members of the class of 2020, there was no pomp, due to the circumstance. She and her classmates had no ceremony to mark the occasion; nor did they attend prom, or enjoy any of the other trivialities or formalities that go with finishing high school. Their freshman year of college this fall promises to be void of the ordinary rituals and milestones, with none of the open-armed welcome to campus and teary drop-offs by parents.

Esmé shouldered the loss of these milestones with aplomb. That's not to say that she didn't acknowledge the truth: This situation sucked. But she could see that others were suffering in ways that were much worse. "I can't be mad at the world for canceling my prom when there are people missing their families, when people are dying," she said. The worst part? The loss of human connection, the inability to say goodbye to school friends and teachers, and the lack of an in-person coda to high school. "I don't care about missing events, as much as the connections those events would have provided. I really missed sharing those final experiences with the rest of my classmates," she told me as we sat in our backyard, on the evening she was supposed to be at her prom.

I often describe my mother and father as having been born during the Great Depression, and coming of age during World War II. Eerily, Esmé's generation is similar to my parents', in that she was born right after 9/11, and is now coming of age during this global pandemic. Her childhood was bookended by these two seminal tragedies, but she and her classmates carried on. I admire this generation, their resilience and positivity in the face of it all. These teenagers have coalesced around hope for a better future; around their shared support for frontline workers; and around marching for social change in this, the strangest summer of their lives.

———

Actually, Esmé will have a graduation ceremony, after all. Planned for August instead of June, it will take place on a computer screen. It will be *virtual*. Everything is virtual now; I've had virtual meetings, virtual chats with friends, virtual presentations to the Parkinson's community.

The Oxford English Dictionary obviously understood that this term needed a new, second definition:

Virtual (Adjective)
1. Almost or nearly as described.
2. In computing: not physically existing as such, but made by software to appear to do so.

Last week I went to a virtual funeral for my very real friend Nanci Ryder. Nanci was my publicist from my earliest days on *Family Ties*. I was her first client, among a long list of famous names to follow. They all loved her as much as I did. Nanci was funny, pushy, loving, terrorizing, and the type of friend you'd want to have your back.

About six years ago, she was diagnosed with amyotrophic lateral sclerosis: ALS. I visited Nanci whenever I was in L.A., along with Tracy or Justine Bateman, who was also a client. We'd sit in her Hollywood Hills living room and retell all the old stories. She could still communicate, though after a while, only with the use of a Boogie Board LCD writing tablet. She would type into it, and her virtual voice enunciated her words. Her sense of humor was still sharp, evidenced as she typed: "Nobody gets my Prada handbags."

Nanci's funeral was held in Los Angeles; I attended from my home in New York. Those gathered at the service were all masked, so that when each appeared in a tiny box on my screen, I couldn't identify the faces, only eyes and muzzled voices. Strange that the good guys wear the masks now.

＝

Collectively, we have witnessed health care professionals, doctors, nurses, and frontline workers, acting as the true heroes in the onslaught of the pandemic. I sheepishly recall my petulance and obstinance in dealing with my home health aides while I recovered from surgery. Now I realize that these same professionals were likely called into service during the darkest days of New York's ordeal, those terrible months of March, April, and May. I'm grateful for all of the brave health care workers in our city and farther afield, with a special acknowledgment to those at Mount Sinai and at Johns Hopkins in Baltimore, for the risks they took and the sacrifices they made.

During our time in quarantine, my family and I would get up from our dinner at 7:00, timed with hospital shift changes, and emerge onto our front porch. We joined our neighbors, isolated in their own bubbles, and we all banged on pots, blew whistles, and rang cowbells in support of health care workers. We could hear the joyful appreciation wafting from the village, down side streets and avenues. A band of thousands, sending a message of thanks out to the universe.

As things stand now, there remains a level of suffering and fear felt by many people: an uncertainty about their living situations, employment security, children's educations, and the outcome to this global problem. For those devastated by loss, I hope that, in time, they will find some peace and resolution. As impossible as it is to imagine, there are fragments of hope in the wreckage, as well as things to be grateful for. Indeed, good things can come from bad things. Many families, ours included, were fortunate to discover unexpected and valued time with one another as we faced this battle together.

We can all take something positive from the class of 2020; to accept what has happened in the past, to embrace the present, and to remain open to the probability that it will get better in the future. I hear echoes of Stephen Pollan in that advice: *With gratitude, optimism becomes sustainable.*

Michael J. Fox
New York City
August 2020

Acknowledgments

Tracy, your love, our family, and the extraordinary life we share, I spill it all and you never censor and never complain. What a wild, wonderful world we've made. You are the fuel that gets me through every day and everything I do. You make all the good things possible. We carry on together and thrive. I love you and can't wait for what comes next.

Sam, make no mistake, I do love you more than Gus. I couldn't ask for a better son, or a better friend to laugh with. Aquinnah, how could someone who works so hard still have the energy to be so funny? You're witty, wise, and winsome. Schuyler, I know you're looking out for me all of the time, and I'm looking out for you. And yes, it would've happened anyway. Esmé, Class of 2020, the last one out of the nest. Let's face it, you got a raw deal, but rose above a tough situation to see the bigger picture. You have spirit, perspective, and smarts.

I love you all, and I love being your Dood.

Mom, I hope you're out of quarantine when you read this. Thank you for teaching me to work hard, and to love everybody. Dad, I still can't believe you drove me to L.A. I feel you with me all the time. Steve, Jackie, Kelli: Thank you for everything. I feel so lucky that we've remained close in spite of the geographic distance between us. I look forward to our family get-togethers, along with Laureen, the kids, and the kids' kids. Karen, you are forever with us.

Stephen Pollan. As I wrote this book, it became clearer to me, and hopefully to the reader, that you will forever be *The Answer Man*. You embodied serenity. Also, like you said, it does get better . . . but it was better when you were here.

Corky, the thoroughly modern matriarch. I've never seen you angry, and I've never seen you sit down. You are a true inspiration, and the best mother-in-law I could ever ask for. Michael and Judith, Lori and Bob, Dana and Mitchell, and the cousins: I know you guys are in my corner, and your love and kindness are appreciated.

Michael Pollan. Sensei. You read the first few pages of this manuscript and expressed enthusiasm and encouragement. I'd check in every few chapters, and you would say, "Keep going." And I did, whilst heeding your buzzwords . . . truth and velocity. I hope you approve.

Thanks to my former assistant—now manager—Nina Tringali. You are always there for me, while at the same time being one step ahead. You really are Radar O'Reilly. My love and gratitude know no bounds. I could not have survived this book or the insanity of the past few years without you. I know the sacrifices you've made, and I thank you.

To Nelle Fortenberry, brilliant friend and longtime producing partner. With our backgrounds in television production, not publishing, we approached this book like we would a film or TV project. You did the heavy lifting, kept us on schedule, handled the research and the business details. You made it work. All I had to do was write. I can't use paper and pen, as my handwriting is scrawl, or use a keyboard because I just tap out Morse code, so I dictated from my notes, which even I couldn't decipher. You managed to type all of this as quickly as I said it, while—and this is the amazing part—listening creatively and critically, and formulating suggestions and ideas about how to shape the material. You not only helped me tell my story to the reader, but you helped tell it to me. This simply would not be a book without you. I am grateful. Love, your partner.

Harlan Coben and George Stephanopoulos, my golf uncles, lunch dates, and treasured friends. What can I say that I haven't said? All the rounds, all the laughs, and the road trips. Unforgettable. Thanks to you both for the book advice, and to Harlan for your invaluable notes and suggestions. Also, love to Anne and the kids, and to Ali, Harper, and Elliott. Cam Neely: Thank you for decades of friendship. Welcome back from the Bubble. I'm sure Paulina, Jack, and Ava are happy to have you home. To Ted Davis: my steadfast, do-or-die, any-weather-any-time golf buddy. Thanks for everything.

Curtis, Carolyn, Ally, Brad, and Jack. It wouldn't be a book without the Schenkers. We're so lucky you're in our lives.

Heartfelt thanks to the talented company of professionals at Flatiron Books, led by Bob Miller, President and Publisher. Bob, your belief in me as an author means a great deal. I appreciated your input on this book, as well as the others; consistently insightful and constructive. Thank you. Let's do it again. For all of your creative contributions and support, my appreciation to Flatiron's Megan Lynch, SVP and Publisher; Emily Walters, Managing Editor; Keith Hayes, Executive Art Director; Cristina Gilbert, VP, Associate Publisher; Marlena Bittner, VP, Director of Publicity; Nancy Trypuc, VP, Director of Marketing; Louis Grilli, Publishing Coordinator; Christopher Smith, Publicity Manager; Lauren Bittrich, Editorial Assistant; and to Michelle McMillian, Associate Director of Design at Macmillan Publishing. Special thanks to the accomplished Guy Oldfield at Macmillan Audio Books.

For embracing this book on the other side of the Atlantic, my gratitude to the UK group at Headline: Sarah Emsley, Publishing Director, Non-Fiction; Lou Swannell, Communications Director; and Fergus Edmondson,

Marketing Director. Thanks also to my UK agent, Gordon Wise at Curtis Brown; and to Helen Manders, for handling the translating markets.

To my literary agent, the legendary Binky Urban. We survived another one. Thank you. And John DeLaney and Sam Fox (not *that* Sam Fox) at ICM, your hard work is greatly appreciated.

To my amazing editor, Leslie Wells. So smart and intuitive. You always understood what I was doing and encouraged me to take chances. Your turnaround time on notes, especially given the pandemic, was most impressive. This is not our first time working together, and it won't be the last.

Leslie Sloane, my tenacious and talented publicist. Sloaney, just tell me where to go, who to talk to, and what to say. Appreciation also to Jami Kandel, who never drops the ball.

Mark Seliger, one of the great photographers of our time. So generous with your art. I am humbled by your loyalty and consistently thrilled by your genius.

Thank you, Ida Biering, for your rapid typing skills and good-natured Danish vibe. We loved working with you.

To my incredible medical team: Dr. Susan Bressman, the one and only. The best. Dr. Rony Shimony, truly the nicest man on the planet. My heart is in good hands. Dr. Leesa Galatz, having you fix my arm was a lucky break. Dr. Nicholas Theodore, I can't thank you enough. I always know you've got my back.

To Joyce A., it's all about "the smoking jacket." With gratitude.

And thanks to Dr. Kim Rosenthal, DVM, for loving Gus as much as we do.

A *healthy* thank you to my physical, occupational, and speech therapists, and to all the others at Johns Hopkins and Mount Sinai who got me moving. A special nod to my PTs—and friends—Ryan Orser and Will Weinrauch, who make sure I keep moving. Thanks also to the skilled home health aides and nurses who put up with me while I healed, and to Akebah and Kenroy for the rides.

The "second act" of my career was filled with meaningful roles and valued friendships. Thank you to Bill Lawrence, David E. Kelley, Larry David, Robert and Michelle King, Julianna Margulies, Kiefer Sutherland, Spike Lee, and Stefon Bristol.

Denis Leary: you're the f***ing hardest working man in f***ing show business. So happy that we got to work together. Even happier that we're friends. And thank you, Ann. Training animals is impressive; putting up with Denis is f***ing heroic.

Seven years ago, I lost my friend and mentor Gary David Goldberg. Gary, none of this would have happened. . . .

Many thanks to my long-standing agents, the sagacious Peter Benedek and the wonderful Nancy Gates. And to Heidi Feigin for getting me out there.

For all things legal, and for being on my side for so many years, my gratitude to Cliff Gilbert-Lurie (who has a surprise cameo in the book) and Jamey Cohen. And to Cole Stephenson for swimming through all the paperwork. Much love to the diligent and dedicated Aaron Philpott, and his impressive team, Amber Hamilton, Vickie Vlahos, and Vincent Araneta. Thanks for taking care of business. Miss you, Bob.

To Keith Richards, Pirate King. Thank you.

Anne Marie Dunleavy and her entire team at Madison Square Garden, thanks for all the special care and consideration.

Mr. K, the turtle swims on. The next time you ink me, it will be Gus.

I am forever grateful to those who keep my life organized and in motion: Amuna Ali, Melida Smith, Noemi Dean, Marielle Kehoe, Caitlin Santora, and Billy Lyons.

And Will Savage for the shoulder.

Jimmy and Cherryl Choi: thanks for sharing your lives with us, first for our film and then for the book. You're both heroes. Karina and Mason are lucky kids.

To the dedicated staff at The Michael J. Fox Foundation for Parkinson's

Research, skillfully led by Co-Founder and Executive Vice Chairman Debi Brooks; and our excellent CEO, Todd Sherer, Ph.D. Thank you both for taking the time to review chapters of this manuscript and for your valuable input. Thanks also to the rest of our expert leadership team: Sohini Chowdhury, Holly Teichholtz, Jim McNasby, Brian Fiske, Ph.D, Mark Frasier, Ph.D, Will Fowler, Michele Golombuski, Jude Williamson, and Ted Thompson, J.D. With your guidance, and the hard work of our valued staff, board members, volunteers, and funders, I know we are destined to find a cure.

About the Author

A professional actor for nearly five decades, MICHAEL J. FOX is also known for his work as an activist, philanthropist, and author. Michael lives with his wife, Tracy Pollan, and good dog, Gus, in New York City, where they enjoy frequent visits from their four adult children.